FAT RABBIT COOKS

Original Recipe Mississippi Cooking

Martha Hellon Pullen

ISBN 978-1-63885-543-9 (Paperback)
ISBN 978-1-63885-545-3 (Hardcover)
ISBN 978-1-63885-544-6 (Digital)

Covenant Books
11661 Hwy 707
Murrells Inlet, SC 29576
www.covenantbooks.com

For my daughter Donnis, and for my grandson Jarrett, who used to say, "Grandma, we need to enter a cooking contest" every other day. I miss them both dearly for always being my cheerleaders. For my sister Barbara and my sister girl Sally, who said, "You have got to. You must write a cookbook before you can't anymore." To my biggest cheerleaders, my husband John and my mama Cordie Mae, from whom I absorbed all that she gladly had to give. My mama always taught me that nothing hurts a failure but a try. One mountain, one step to living life lively.

CONTENTS

ACKNOWLEDGMENTS

God for strength and determination.

For my Mama, Cordie Mae McDade, who has always reminded me that no matter what the circumstances or influences around you, be kind and do your best because truly 'nothing hurts a failure but a try.' My aunts, Velma and Hattie Lee, who always took the time to teach me what they knew and never gave up on me.

Thank you to all my friends and family who have stayed on my nerves about putting together my recipes in a book. Special thanks to my sister girl, Sally Heard Turner, who refused to stop reminding me year after year to do this for the family. She never stopped trying to encourage me even when I dismissed her numerous times. Sally and her daughter, Meka Turner, also helped with my introduction.

My best friend, Shirley Queen, who for over forty years has always positively reenforced all things that had to do with me without judgment or criticism. I thank her for testing so many dishes and reminding me that everyone does not know what a 'little of this and a little of that' means. Since I rarely measure anything, she made sure I got to see a real teaspoon of salt. Whew. Got it.

My granddaughter, Jazmine Eitson, who assisted John with taking sometimes ten or twenty pictures of whatever dish I made to get the best possible view. She is also my second taster in charge.

My cousin, Al Rogers, for making me feel guilty for not writing instructions down and encouraging me weekly with hints and ideas. And to his lovely wife, Carol Rogers, for the beautiful towels, kitchen accessories, and aprons she made to include as backdrop for some of my pictures. To all my family and friends that also prepared several dishes and sent pictures and comments about their results, adding comments, and seeking clarification when necessary.

And to my husband, John Pullen, who is my chief taster in charge, for graciously taking on the burden of tasting and eating everything I cook and for taking on the responsibility of all the things that I neglected during this journey. I love you so much. And God willing, get ready for our next project, an Inspirational CD and book titled *The Hardest Thing.*

INTRODUCTION

My mama taught me to always be happy with whatever God blessed us with, even if it is less than we anticipated. We were always glad no matter what we got. Mama could change almost anything into something good, especially a meal.

This is for the friends and family that say they love my cooking and asked me many times to share my recipes. I use readily available ingredients and mostly name brand sauce and condiments. I love cooking for everybody and tend to stick with tried-and-true recipes. Recipes are perfected by knowing when *not* to add any more seasonings. I learned to cook with a pinch of this and a pinch of that. I have tried to give you better measurements. I do hope this makes them want to try out new recipes and find joy in cooking all the things that make family eating and sharing great. Most recipes are family favorites, the way I learned to cook. I have also included some of my favorites, which I have designated as Martha's.

When I was a little girl, my grandfather Marvin nicknamed me Fat Rabbit, which everyone called me since then. Do not know why really. I knew I was a little different from the other kids. I liked hanging around the older folks to listen to their stories. Because of that, whatever they were snacking on, I always got some, so I was short and chubby. No matter who was cooking, I was usually in the kitchen watching, trying to help out or tasting. If anybody made a cake, I got the bowl. My uncle Heard used to cook different stuff, and his favorite was brains and eggs. Of course, I was there to observe and taste. Aunt Velma baked mostly cakes, but every Sunday, she would make a pot roast with potatoes with a side of corn. Mama cooked everything. So I watched everybody. Okay, I know why they called me Fat Rabbit!

I started cooking just about everything I knew at that time when I was about twelve. My mama worked evenings so she would start cooking something for dinner for me to finish. She said that when she was about eight, she and her sister Velma would get up early to cook for my grandfather who worked at the railroad. She said she loved frying okra and green tomatoes and loved cooking. She also loved eating peas one at time. Her father and her brother both encouraged their cooking, so they just kept trying. Aunt Velma made the sweets, while Mama cooked the vegetables. It seems to me that whatever was on hand, my aunts and mama made them into different and distinct dishes.

My mother could cook just about anything. She worked as a prep person in a French restaurant in Milwaukee for years. After that, she was a short-order cook at a huge bar, then as a line cook at a hospital. Everything she cooked tasted so much better than anyone else's cooking it seemed like. She loved her vegetables and corn bread. Every dish had corn bread served with it. All green vegetables were cooked to perfection. Most people would cook their fresh greens for an hour or more, but Mama's would be done in twenty minutes. She was quick at making meals. She did not like mushy vegetables or meat. Tender is good, but food should still have a bite to it.

My mother and my aunt Velma loved crappies, bluegill, chicken wings, and the bony part of meats. They both hated milk, eggs, and butter because they had to tend to the chickens and the cows, gathering eggs and churning butter. Aunt Hattie was the oldest girl, so she did not have run after them because of her asthma. Mama, Aunt Hattie, and Aunt Velma would always congregate at one of their kitchen tables to nibble something and drink coffee. Everyone always had a saucer with a little of this or that. They never got a piece of cake, just a thin slice multiple times. My mama always talked about how my grandmother Helen loved butter rolls and bread pudding. Mama hated it. She said it was because they had to work collecting eggs and milking cows that she did not want anything made with it. I asked her how to make it to add to list of recipes. She still does not even want to taste the dish, though most folks remember it fondly.

My aunt Hattie was a classy lady. Nothing seemed to faze her. I remember she made the best jellies and a great custard pie. When I went to her house, me and my cousins would toast a whole loaf of bread and slathered them with homemade jelly. She was good in the kitchen, but she did not cook as much as Mama and Aunt Velma. She left the cooking to Uncle Heard. Uncle Heard made the best homemade ice cream. If I was at their house, I was in the kitchen. I remember that Aunt Thelma, the youngest sister, would always pick the greens, cleaning each leaf with a towel. Quite a few Southern women added the towel step when picking greens. While Aunt Thelma did all the prep work, Uncle Otlee did most of the cooking in their house, and he was pretty good at it. My aunt Maggie always made the pound cakes, which she dusted with powdered sugar. She loved sharing her knowledge about cooking and making the most beautiful quilts. As much as I love sewing, I did not get into quilting.

We used to go to Mississippi every year, sometimes twice a year. It was like another country. For whatever reason, I was smart enough not to judge, but I was glad to get back home after every trip. It was so hot there. In a lot of ways, I think they had it so good. People without stoves and refrigerators seemed to be able to do so much more with much less than I thought we had. You would not believe what my folks could cook on wood stoves—such as cakes and pies, baked sweet potatoes and roast corn—without burning! I myself need temperature checks and timers in the kitchen. Everybody had a garden with the prettiest greens, okra, squash, green beans, pole beans, tomatoes, and corn, even if they only had a small plot. Whatever was in the garden was usually prepared for the table. In the evening, someone would always serve a watermelon, and everyone would have a piece, so good and sweet.

The very first time I had fried chicken for breakfast was in Water Valley, Mississippi, at my Aunt Eppie's house. We were invited for supper, which was really early to me, at about 2:00 p.m. There was so much food on that table that I thought, *Oh my, these folks are rich.* I had never been anywhere with that much food in one place, even during holidays meals at home. Keep in mind that back in those days, we did not go to restaurants or had McDonalds. We had peas, greens, sliced tomatoes, freshly made sausage, biscuits, corn bread, fried chicken, corn on the cob, green beans, potatoes, and fried apples. There were yams, homemade jams and jellies, chowchow, and pound cake. Heaven! I remember that Aunt Steppa, which is what everyone called Aunt Eppie, had guineas, chickens, cows, and more turkeys than I had ever seen. It sounded like all of them were squawking at the same time.

You cannot talk about Mississippi without mentioning Couzin Lucille. I used to love to hear her holler for the kids to come home to dinner. It seemed you could hear her all over Bruce, Mississippi. Lucille was the first woman I knew who owned and operated a business. During those years, we couldn't wait to get there. It was the only restaurant we were able to go to. Years later, I knew with certainty that this was a monumental achievement, having a determined Black woman in charge of her own business.

I learned a few things I have always tried to share. Most people have their own way of preparing any dish and have a hard time trying something different no matter what. I have been asked more times than I can count how to make a dish, but often someone would tell you how they do it before you could even finish trying to explain it. How can you possibly learn a new method if you do not follow the instructions that you ask for? Whenever I try out a new recipe, I will follow the directions. Then, if I wanted to, I would tweak it after tasting the original results.

LITTLE TIPS

- Always add a pinch of salt to sweet recipes.
- A pinch of salt and sugar will enhance most recipes. You don't need a lot.
- Always parboil meat that you are not frying or roasting; for instance, neck bones or beef bones or oxtails. This will remove the need to skim the scum.
- I wash almost everything, including lettuce, before I put it in the spinner with cold water and a pinch of salt. Then spin dry.
- When using canned good—tomatoes, chili beans, etc.—always empty into a bowl or pan to check that there are no bad pieces before adding to your pot.
- Before cooking any meat, except steak, I wash it and then let it sit in a little salt water for 5 minutes. The meat will not be salty.
- Steaks to be grilled are washed and put straight on the grill. If I oven grill the steaks, I marinate them first.
- Bleach is a must. Always wash up with bleach after handling chicken. Keep your surfaces clean and do not use the same utensils for other foods.
- Always keep a stone or earthenware jar to collect bacon grease or leftover salt pork grease. The grease keeps well but discard and renew if it starts to smell rank.
- If you have one smile a day, spend it at home.

KITCHEN STAPLES

- Sometimes brand does matter.
- Hellman's mayonnaise
- Kraft Sandwich Spread
- PET milk
- Henri's Tas-Tee dressing (available at Amazon)
- Crushed and whole red pepper (dry)
- Apple cider vinegar
- Ro-Tel tomatoes
- Petite Diced and crushed tomatoes
- Worcestershire sauce
- Nutmeg
- Cinnamon
- Whole cloves
- Penzeys Fox Point seasoning
- Bouillon cubes, chicken and beef
- Eagle Brand milk
- Onion
- Green pepper
- Poultry seasoning
- White Lily self-rising flour
- Celery
- Dry beans
- Jasmine rice

PICKING FRESH GREENS

When you shop for greens, always try to get the greenest, freshest vegetables possible. The greens should not be bone dry or brittle to the touch and be free of brown spots. Any size is okay if it's fresh. Sometimes if greens have been water sprayed too much at the market, they will have dark spots or a mushy feel. If the greens have too many bug or wormholes, look for another bunch. When you pick through the greens, check for bugs or worms, tears, or pinched-off bad spots. If the leaf is too buggy, discard.

If you can find them, it is best if you pick fresh greens from the garden. Strip the large tough center stem from each leaf, leaving a piece toward the top of the leaf. Some stem is good. Wash the greens in cold water. The first washing should have 1 tablespoon of salt and a drop of dish liquid. Change to clean water until there is no grit left in the water.

For *turnips*, after picking and washing them, tear the greens a little.

For *collards*, after washing them, stack, roll, and cut into thin strips.

Mama picking fresh greens

PREPARING SEASONING STOCK FOR VEGETABLES

1 good size piece of old country ham plus 2 or 3 smoked ham hocks
2 or 3 ½ inch thick slices of salt pork. Cut along the top edge, but not thru the skin.

Cooking ham hock and old meat is simply boiling and rendering flavor from the smoked meat. Divide for multiple cooking. Wash 2 or 3 smoked ham hocks.

Render (fry until grease is cooked out) salt pork slowly in the pot you will be cooking in. A large boiling pot is best. Add at least 3 quarts of water. Add ham hock and ham or old meat and cook until all are rendered and the hocks are tender. Cook low and slow so you do not evaporate all the liquid out. Make sure that the pot does not boil too fast. You should have 2 quarts of liquid left. This cooking should be enough to season a few pots of vegetables. When seasoning greens, I always render a couple pieces salt pork until all the grease is out.

HOW TO CURE SALT PORK

4 or 5 pkg. of 1 lb. salt pork
1 lb. pack pork jowl

Buy salt pork that has a streak of lean meat or two in it. You do not want too much lean, but a little is essential. Cut salt pork in to 1/2 inch slices.

Get a clean cardboard box. Layer of few pieces of newspaper in the bottom of the box. Put a layer of aluminum foil on top of the newspaper. Put several layers of wax paper on the foil. Lay the slices of salt pork on wax paper. Sprinkle salt on one side, turn it, and salt the other side. Put another layer of salt pork and sprinkle with salt. It is okay if they are touching as long as it is not packed. Once all the slices have some salt on them, put a piece of wax paper over them and another piece of foil. Close the box and put in the garage or attic, wherever it is hottest. Leave for a few weeks. It will dry out slightly. This is fine.

I cure most of my pork in the summer and then freeze it. Wash before using. It will be a little greasy, and it's okay to have a little salt left on them.

PARBOILING MEATS

Whenever you cook meats that will be boiled, except for *corned beef,* you must parboil the meat to remove the scummy liquid first. When you parboil meats, you can start from frozen without thawing first. Add enough water to almost cover the meat. You do not need to completely cover to start because as the meat gets hot, you can move the bones around so that everything is covered. Heat the water to boiling and make sure the meat is submerged with enough water to parboil all the meat.

Always start with a clean scrubbed sink so you can pour the water and the meat into the sink. Trim the fat and membrane from the bones. Wash thoroughly and clean the pot that you used. Now season it and add vegetables to your meat to continue your recipe.

APPETIZERS

Hog's Head Cheese and Deviled Eggs

Deviled Eggs

4 large boiled eggs
1/2 tsp. yellow mustard
1/2 tsp. spicy mustard
1 tsp. pickle relish
1 tbsp. mayo
1 tbsp. sandwich spread
a pinch of salt and pepper

Cover eggs with cold water in a saucepan. Add 1 tablespoon of salt. When water starts to boil, time and cook for 10 minutes. Rinse in cold water and peel. Cut each egg in half lengthwise carefully. Remove yolks into small bowl. Mash slightly. Add all other ingredients and mix well. Put mixture by the spoonful into each egg half. Sprinkle with paprika and chill. Serve with a cold plate or eat as a snack.

Hog's Head Cheese or Souse

6 or 7 lbs. of pig's feet (or 8 whole feet)
1 pig tail
1 small neck bone
3 tbsp. crushed red pepper (adjust for heat)
2 or 3 tsp. rubbed sage
1/2 tsp. cayenne pepper
3/4 c. white vinegar
2 stalks of celery
1/2 onion
1 whole red chili pepper
1/2 lemon
1/4 c. cooking liquid from pig's feet (Do not discard final cooking liquid until all done.)
salt
pepper

Wash all meat. Cut up the pig's feet if whole or ask the butcher to do it. Most times, the feet are sold in small pieces. Parboil, drain, and wash, cutting away any bad pieces. Replace the pot with fresh water with 2 teaspoon of salt and 1 teaspoon of pepper. Add celery, lemon, whole pepper and onion to pot. Cook meat slowly until falling off the bone, about 21/2 to 3 hours.

After removing the skin, remove the lean meat that is under the skin next to the bone. Put in the pan you are going to make the hog's head cheese in. Take the meat and skin off the pig's feet and tail. Remove all the meat from neck bone and add to the pan. If you use a pig's ear, chop it up as finely as you can. It is a little tricky because the skin will come off and the ear tends to be a little harder to chop because it is cartilage.

After taking all the meat from them, discard the, bones. You may wear plastic gloves if you like because the meat and juice is very sticky. Mash the meat with your fingers to get all the bones out. You must do this twice just to be sure there are no small bones. When you are satisfied that you have removed all the bones, mash the meat with a potato masher. Add seasonings and vinegar. Stir and taste. Add 1/4 cup of cooking liquid and stir. Save 1/2 cup of liquid just in case. (A little cooking liquid is good, but I use more vinegar.) Adjust the salt. Pour into an 8 x 8 or 9 x 9 inch pan.

Refrigerate. If the seasoning is not quite right for you, you can heat the cheese until it just liquefies. Adjust your seasoning and refrigerate again. I cut mine into three-by-nine-inch sections and freeze until ready to use. *Do not microwave.* Just bring them down to room temperature or thaw in the refrigerator.

Salsa

2 large fresh tomatoes, chopped
1/2 c. chopped cilantro
2 tbsp. lime juice
1/2 c. chopped green onion (white and green)
1/2 c. sweet onion, chopped
1 jalapeño pepper, chopped (stems and ribs removed)
1/2 tsp. sea salt
1/2 tsp. cracked pepper
1 tbsp. sugar

Wash and dry cilantro on paper towels. Chop the tomatoes and onions. Remove stem, ribs, and seeds from jalapeños and thinly cut into small circles. Mix all vegetables together. Blend in lime juice, salt, pepper, and sugar. Mix all ingredients together and chill thoroughly. Adjust seasonings if needed.

SALADS

Chicken Salad

1/2 c. sweet pickle juice
2 c. chopped chicken breast
1 c. mayo
1/2 finely chopped sweet onion
2 boiled eggs, chopped
1 c. thinly sliced celery
2 chopped large sweet pickles
2 tsp. sugar
1/4 tsp. salt

Parboil and rinse chicken breasts, removing cartilage and skin. Cut each breast in half as equally as possible so that it cooks evenly. Simmer in boiling salted water for about 20 minutes. Cool until easily handled. Cut into small chunks. Pour pickle juice over the chicken and drain. Add onion, chopped pickle, eggs, and celery. Mix lightly. Combine sugar, salt, mayo, and 1 teaspoon of pickle juice or lemon juice. Add mixture to the chicken mixture to lightly bind. Chill until ready to serve.

This is good with croissants or crackers. I usually serve a scoop with green salad.

Coleslaw

1/2 large cabbage cut into fine strips or one bag of angel hair coleslaw
1 large carrot, shredded
1/2 c. whipping cream
1/2 c. mayo
1/2 tsp. salt
3 tbsp. sugar
2 tbsp. lemon juice
1/4 c. Henri's Tas-Tee dressing

Remove the outer leaves from cabbage and wash. Cut into quarters and remove the core. Cut the core like making a triangle piece with the bottom being the base. On the cutting board, shred the cabbage with a sharp knife by laying a section on its side and starting to slice thin strips. Two quarters of cabbage will make enough slaw for four or five people.

Meanwhile, peel and shred the carrot with a grater. Combine all ingredients together in a large bowl. Taste and adjust seasoning. Refrigerate for about an hour. The slaw will have more juice after it is chilled. You need to stir again before serving.

I like a sweet, creamy slaw. If you cannot find Tas-Tee, try a coleslaw dressing.

Corn Salad

2 ears of corn cut fresh from the cob
1 tbsp. butter
1/2 red or Vidalia onion, sliced
1 green onion, slice thinly
1 large fresh tomato
1/2 large cucumber, sliced
1/2 small jalapeño pepper
1/2 c. Italian dressing
2 tbsp. of Splenda

Cut corn from the cob. Using a sharp knife, cut two thin layers of corn and then scrape the remaining corn from the cob. Sauté pepper and green onion in butter until it just starts to simmer. Add corn. Simmer for 2 more minutes and remove from heat. Chill.

Cut onion and cucumber into thin slices. Slice tomato in slightly thicker slices than the onion and cucumber. Layer on serving dish with cucumber at the bottom of the dish. Mix Italian dressing with Splenda and stir until well combined. Spoon over layered tomato mixture. Serve chilled with tomato mixture on top of lettuce or butter lettuce on plate. Spoon chilled corn over each serving.

Cranberry Fluff Salad

1 12 oz. bag of fresh cranberries (not canned)
1 c. sugar
1 fresh red apple
11/2 cups peeled seedless red grapes
1/2 bag of small marshmallows
1 c. pecans
2 packages of Dream Whip
1/2 c. milk
1/2 tsp. vanilla

Wash and drain the cranberries. Chop up in blender coarsely, but do not mash. Cover cranberries with sugar and refrigerate overnight. (Cranberries can be prepared ahead and frozen for up to 6 months). Drain cranberries after they are sugared.

Peel and dice the apple into 1/2 inch pieces. Peel the grapes and cut in half. Break pecans into large pieces and warm in oven for 4 to 5 minutes until fragrant. Mix all ingredients except milk, vanilla, and Dream Whip together.

Put a small mixing bowl and mixer beaters in the freezer for a few minutes to chill. When cold, add 2 packs of Dream Whip to 1/2 cup of milk and 1/2 teaspoon of vanilla in the bowl. Whip until stiff. Add whipped Dream Mix to cranberry mixture. Add additional marshmallows if a little soupy. Chill until ready to serve. Serve with corn bread dressing instead of cranberry sauce.

Cucumber Salad

2 cucumbers
1/2 tsp. salt
1/2 tsp. black pepper
1 tsp. sugar
1 tsp. lemon juice
1 stalk of celery
1/4 small onion
mayo

Wash and peel cucumbers. Slice thinly and put slices on a plate. Sprinkle with salt and set aside for 15 minutes. Drain. Slice the onion and celery thinly and mix with cucumber. Sprinkle with a little squeeze of lemon juice. Mix all other ingredients together, starting with about 3 tablespoons of mayo (may need more as binder). Mix cucumbers lightly with mayo mixture and chill. Serve with cocktail bread as an appetizer or on toasted white bread and tea sandwiches.

Egg Salad

3 boiled eggs, chopped
2 tbsp. sandwich spread
1 tbsp. mayo
1 tbsp. relish
1 tbsp. finely chopped celery
1 tsp mustard
sprinkle of red pepper or drop of hot sauce

Put eggs in cold water and add 1 teaspoon salt. Bring to a boil. Set timer for 10 minutes after start of the boil. After 10 minutes, take out the eggs and run cold water over them. Peel and let it cool. Dice the eggs and mix with all the ingredients. Chill until ready to serve.

Hot Bacon Dressing

1/2 c. sugar
1/2 tsp. salt
2 tbsp. cornstarch
1 egg, well beaten
1/4 c. white vinegar
1 c. water
1/4 lb. fried bacon, chopped

Mix sugar, salt, and cornstarch together. Beat egg and add to the water. Mix well. Add the egg mixture to the dry ingredients slowly until it is smooth. Add vinegar and cook on medium high until mixture is thick.

Fry or bake bacon until crisp. Crumble when cool enough to handle. Add bacon to dressing, stir, and serve over lettuce wedge or a combination of crispy lettuce and spinach while the dressing is still warm.

Macaroni Salad

3 cups of cooked elbow macaroni

1/2 cucumber, peeled and sliced (sprinkle with salt for a few minutes first and then drain)

1/2 c. grape tomatoes

1/4 c. thinly sliced red onion

1/4 c. thinly sliced green pepper

1/4 c. thinly sliced red pepper

1/2 tsp. sea salt

1/2 tsp. cracked black pepper

1/4 tsp. red pepper flakes

4 hard-boiled eggs, chopped

1/2 c. diced sweet pickle

1 tbsp. sugar

1/2 c. mayo

1/2 c. Tas-Tee dressing

Combine all ingredients. Cool in refrigerator at least a few hours. Stir again before serving. Adjust seasonings. Add more mayo or Tas-Tee dressing if needed.

SALADS

Potato Salad and Slaw

34

Potato Salad

8 small red potatoes (1 1/2 to 3 inch)
3 sweet pickles, chopped
3 boiled eggs, chopped
1/2 stick of celery stalk, thinly sliced
1/4 c finely chopped green pepper
1 tbsp. yellow mustard
1 tbsp. Dijon or brown mustard
2 tbsp. sugar
1/2 tsp. salt
2/3 c. mayo (adjust as needed depending on size of potatoes)
1/2 c. Henri's Tas-Tee dressing (If you cannot find the dressing, add more mayo and mustard.)

Cook potatoes until they are tender but not mushy. Cool in refrigerator for best results. You do not want the potatoes to mash when they are too hot. Combine mustard, mayo, Tas-Tee dressing, salt, sugar, and a sprinkle of black pepper. Mix together in a mixing bowl until smooth. Add all other ingredients to the potatoes and combine with the mayo mixture. Use more mayo if necessary. Sprinkle with paprika and top with one boiled egg. Chill or serve at room temperature but refrigerate immediately after serving.

Quick Pasta Salad (Sweet and Sour)

1 c. macaroni, uncooked
1/2 green pepper
1/2 red pepper
1/4 red onion
1 stalk of celery
2 or 3 sweet pickles, chopped
2 tbsp. sugar (Splenda is better here)
1/2 tsp. sea salt
1/2 tsp. crushed red pepper
1 c. Italian dressing, well shaken

Cook macaroni *al dente*. Drain and cool slightly. Cut the pepper and onions into small thin rings. Dice the pickles. Slice celery diagonally into strips the same size as the peppers. All vegetables should be sliced thinly. Mix all ingredients together in bowl. Mix in macaroni and pour dressing over it. Mix until well covered. Chill for at least 2 hours.

Tuna Salad

2 cans Bumble Bee Prime Fillet tuna
1/2 c. sandwich spread
1/2 c. mayo
1/2 c. sweet pickle
4 boiled eggs
1/4 tsp. salt
1/4 tsp. pepper
1 tbsp. finely minced sweet onion

I use water-packed tuna and prefer white fillets. After opening the can, leave the lid in place and run a little water on top. Drain. (It is a Martha thing) Break up the tuna with a fork and then add the rest of the ingredients in a bowl. Mix well. Add more sandwich spread if needed and chill.

Tomato, Cucumber, and Onion Salad

1 large sliced tomato

1 cucumber

1/2 red onion or sweet onion, sliced

1 green onion, thinly sliced

1/2 c. Italian dressing

1/4 c. Splenda sugar (regular sugar is okay but does not work as well)

1/4 to 1/2 tsp. crushed red pepper

1/4 tsp. sea salt

Slice the tomato and cucumber thickly but the onion thinly. Layer in a shallow bowl. Mix dressing with Splenda, red pepper, and sea salt. Pour over sliced veggies and then add the thinly sliced green onion. Refrigerate at least an hour to meld flavors. Serve as a cold side dish.

SOUPS

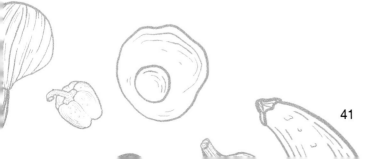

Chili

1 lb. ground beef
1 large onion
1 can Bush pinto chili beans
1/4 c. chili powder
1 package of French's chili powder
1/4 tsp. baking soda
1/2 tsp. cinnamon

I use French's because it also has a little thickener and I like the taste of it better. If you want a chili that is spicier, use more chili powder.

Brown ground beef and sauté with onion. Add 1/2 cup of chopped celery if desired. Add tomatoes, beans, and chili powders. Sir until well blended and cook until the seasonings have mellowed. Add baking soda and cinnamon. Stir and simmer for a while. Remove from heat and serve with sour cream and crackers or corn bread.

The baking soda will stop the indigestion that sometimes comes with eating chili.

Potato Soup

4 stalks of celery, sliced
1 onion, diced
1/2 c. of chopped parsley
5 large yellow potatoes
6 or 8 slices of bacon crisp
4 c. chicken broth
3 chicken bouillon cubes (in addition to broth)
1 c. heavy cream
2 tbsp. flour
1 tbsp. cornstarch
1 tsp. crushed red pepper
1 ear of fresh cob (cut off the cob) optional
1 tsp. black pepper
1 tsp. sugar (optional)

Fry bacon until rendered and crisp tender. Remove bacon and drain. With remaining bacon grease, sauté celery and onion for 2 minutes. Add diced medium potatoes to pot. Stir. Add chicken bouillon cubes and chicken broth. Simmer until potatoes are tender. Add pepper and red pepper flakes. Make a smooth paste of cream, flour, and cornstarch. Temper with a little broth and add to pot. Add fresh corn if using. Simmer for 10 minutes. Add 2 slices cooked crumbled bacon. Add parsley and green onions until heated through. Sprinkle remaining bacon on top of the soup when serving.

VEGETABLES

Baked Beans

1 20 oz. can of baked beans
1/2 c. ketchup
1/4 c. syrup
1/2 c. chopped onion
1 tsp. mustard
2 slices of bacon

Use a pan or casserole deep enough to hold baked beans. Add bacon and bake in the oven at 350 degrees F until crisp. Remove the bacon and mix all other all ingredients together in casserole. Crumble bacon and mix into beans. Baked in the oven for 30 minutes. Serve hot or room temperature.

Boiled Cabbage

1 head of cabbage (I prefer loose-leaf flat head)
2 slices of salt pork
1/2 cup ham hock juice
1/2 red pepper
3 tbsp. sugar
1/2 tsp. salt

Wash and cut up the cabbage. Soak the cabbage in water with 3 or 4 tablespoon of baking soda for 4 or 5 minutes. Drain. Fry the salt pork to render fat. Add red pepper and the cabbage. Stir until cabbage wilts slightly and then add ham hock juice. The cabbage will make some water so just stir until covered with juices from the pot. Add sugar, stir, and cover to cook for 5 to 10 minutes. It will not take long. The baking soda also tenderizes the greens. Turn off the pot. The cabbage will continue to cook if the pot is hot, so do not be tempted to leave the heat on.

Cheese Grits Baked

1 Kraft garlic cheese roll
1 c. of cooked grits
1 stick of butter
2 eggs
1/4 tsp. salt

Cook the grits per package directions. Combine the cooked grits with cheese and butter until well mixed. Beat the eggs lightly. Beat in salt with a hand mixer. Combine grits with eggs in casserole dish or jelly roll pan and bake at 350 degrees F for 30 to 45 minutes. Serve hot.

Mixed Peas, Neck Bones and Corn

Black-Eyed Peas or Mixed Peas

1 bag of frozen black-eyed peas
1 bag of frozen butter peas
2 ham hocks or 2 c. ham hock liquid
2 slices of salt pork
1/2 tsp. salt
1/2 red pepper, crushed
2 tsp. bacon grease

Inspect the peas for foreign matter, wash them, and then set aside. Fry salt pork in the same pot that the peas will be cooked in. Put the peas in the pot after the pork has rendered (fat is fried off) and stir the peas well. Add enough ham hock liquid to the peas and seasonings. Cook for 1 hour. Mash some of the peas against the side of the pot and stir again. Cook for an additional 15 minutes. Mash and stir again. The juice from the peas should be thicken when you stir in the mashed peas.

Collard Greens

2 bunches of collards
2 tbsp. sugar
1 c. old meat liquid (see seasoning meat)
3 tbsp. baking soda (for last wash)
3 tbsp. lard
3 tbsp. bacon or salt pork grease

Pick and wash collard greens thoroughly, until all grit is out. After washing, stack a few green leaves at a time and roll them. Cut the green leaves into strips of 1/4 or 1/2 inch thick and soak in water mixed with 3 heaping tablespoons of baking soda. Let the greens sit for no more than 5 minutes, otherwise they will get mushy.

Render 1 or 2 pieces of salt pork and/or bacon in pot large enough to hold the greens. After the meat is cooked, add a dried red pepper and the drained greens a handful at a time. Stir well. When all the greens all have been added, sprinkle 2 tablespoons of sugar and 3 tablespoons of lard. Keep stirring. Then add a cup at a time of the ham hock juice, stirring after the first cup until almost covered. The greens should wilt down some before adding hot liquid. Cook for about 10 minutes. Taste for desired doneness. Greens will get tender based on its freshness and the length of the soda soak.

I only cook my greens about 10–15 minutes. Remember that they will continue to cook in a hot pot. If the greens are old, they might take a little longer. If you cook too long, they tend to turn color, and the flavor is not the same.

Fried Corn

2 slice of bacon or 1 thin slice of salt pork
1/2 tsp. salt
1 tsp. sugar
1/2 tbsp. flour
1 tbsp. water
1 tbsp. butter
6 ears of fresh corn (corn husks should be bright green and silk pale yellow)

Shuck the corn and remove silk from the cobs. Rinse them well. Cut corn kernels off of the cob using a sharp knife. Place cob in a swallow pan topside up. Hold on to a piece of the top and gently cut a thin line down all the way around. Go around again with another thin section. Now scrap the cob by positioning the knife against the cob and scraping down. Do this all around for each cob. You should have a few cups of fresh cob with the juices or cream that naturally comes from scraping the corn, ready to use.

Fry bacon or salt pork until rendered. This should provide about a tablespoon of fat. Add corn, salt, pepper, and flour. Stir, add water, and cover. Simmer over low heat, stirring occasionally. Cover the pan after each stir. Be careful not to have the skillet or pan heat up too much so the corn does not stick. After 15 minutes, add sugar and butter. Cook for another few minutes and take off the heat. Most of the liquid should be absorbed.

Fried Green Tomatoes

fresh green tomatoes
1/2 c. white meal
1/2 c. flour
1/2 tsp. salt
1/2 tsp. pepper
1 tbsp. oil
1 tbsp. butter

Make sure tomatoes are firm but not hard. Do not peel. Remove the dark stem by cutting a narrow circle at the top and a then cut a thin slice from the bottom. Cut tomatoes into 1/4 inch slices and rub them with salt. Set aside for a few minutes.

Mix meal and flour with pepper. Dredge tomatoes in flour mixture until covered on both sides. Heat oil and butter together until hot. Add the tomatoes to hot oil and fry until golden on one side. Turn and brown on the other side. Drain and serve.

Fried Okra

fresh firm okra
1/2 c. meal
1 tbsp. flour
1/2 tsp. salt
1/2 tsp. cayenne pepper
oil

Wash and rinse the okra. Drain and pat dry. Cut into 1/4 or 1/2 inch slices. The smaller the slices, the better the crunch.

Mix flour, meal, salt, and cayenne together into a dry bowl. Heat an inch of oil in skillet until hot enough to sizzle a pinch of flour. If flour just sits in oil, it is not hot enough. You can also deep fry. Some folks like to dip okra into buttermilk or milk before adding to the flour mixture. Fry several pieces at a time without crowding the skillet. Turn okra when it starts to brown on one side after a few minutes. Continue to fry until golden brown on all sides. Remove from heat and place on paper towels. Serve hot.

Fried Sweet Potatoes

2 tbsp. Crisco
1 large sweet potato
3 tbsp. sugar
2 tbsp. butter
a sprinkle of cinnamon

Peel and slice potatoes in 1/4 or 1/2 inch slices. Melt Crisco and add potatoes to skillet in a single layer. Cover. Brown slowly and turn over to brown the other side. After turning, sprinkle potatoes with sugar and cinnamon. Add a pat of butter and turn. Sprinkle a little more sugar on top and cover. Cook until tender. Serve hot or cold.

Green Beans and Potatoes

fresh green beans or 1 bag of frozen beans
fresh ear of corn
3 or 4 red potatoes
2-inch chunk of old ham or 2 slices of salt pork
1 tsp. salt
1 tbsp. sugar
1 dried red pepper
1 tbsp. bacon grease
1 cup ham hock juice (if you have some)

Trim end and snap green beans. Wash well. Drain and wash again but add 1 tablespoon of baking soda to the water. Swish and then drain. Fry the ham and salt pork slowly on low heat until the grease has rendered in the pot. Add bacon grease and turn up the heat. Add drained beans to the pot and shake to coat with the grease. Add ham hock juice if you have it some or plain water. Add salt, sugar, and red pepper.

Break corn into two pieces and tuck into the cooking liquid. Peel and wash potatoes and lay them on top of the beans. Cover and cook until done.

If you have *fresh green beans from the garden*, just wash them and fry with bacon grease or a little butter. Add sugar and salt and sauté for 10 minutes.

Grilled Corn

6 to 8 ears of fresh corn
1 c. salt
water

Pull stalks back about 2 inches from the top of the cob. Pull off the top part of the silks and cut off any bad tops. Recover the corn with the stalks and tie a sting around the tops to hold it together. Submerge the corn in water in a pot or tub, depending on the amount of corn you are grilling. Add salt. Cover with heavy foil and lay something heavy on top to keep the corn submerged. Soak for a couple of hours or overnight.

Remove corn from the water and lay on top of the grill opposite the fire. The corn will be wet, which is fine. Let it smoke on the hot grill for about 20 to 30 minutes or until done. Dip in melted butter. Allow 2 ears per person.

Onion Rings

1 sweet or white onion, sliced
1 tsp. baking powder
1 tsp. salt
1/2 tsp. black pepper
1/2 tsp. red pepper
1 c. flour
1 tbsp. cornstarch
1/2 c. cold beer or white soda
1 tsp. oil

Mix all dry ingredients together and stir in 1/2 cup of beer. If you do not have one, use 7 Up or a Sprite. Add 1 teaspoon of oil to batter. If too thick, thin with a little extra beer or soda. Heat oil in deep skillet or deep fryer. Add rings to batter to cover and then immediately add to hot oil. Do not crowd too much. You will probably need 2 or 3 batches. Drain on paper towels.

Pan-Fried Squash

My aunt Hattie loved fresh squash. The last time she came to visit, we had a garden. As anybody knows, squash just keeps on giving, so it was fresh and tender. I cooked my aunt some squash as much as she wanted, and everybody helped her eat it.

1 small squash
2 tbsp. oil or butter
2 tbsp. meal
1 tbsp. flour
1/2 tsp. baking powder
salt
pepper

Wash fresh squash and dry it. Slice squash into rounds at desired thickness. Sprinkle with salt and pepper on both sides. Put meal, flour, baking powder in a dish or shallow pan. Coat the squash in the meal mixture on both sides. Heat oil until hot but not smoking. Add squash in a single layer and brown on each side. Serve hot.

Pickled Beets

3 fresh medium beets (about 3)
2 tbsp. of pickling spice
1 bay leaf
1/2 c. apple cider vinegar
3/4 c. sugar
1/2 c. water

Wash the beets. Cut off the leafy stems, leaving about a 1/2 inch of stem on both ends. Wrap the beets in heavy aluminum foil. Bake in the oven at 350 degrees F for about an hour until just tender. Let it cool. Once cooled, the beets should be peel easily. Peel and slice. Put the beets into saucepan and add remaining ingredients. Liquid should just cover beets. Simmer slowly for an hour. Serve hot or chilled.

Sautéed Spinach

1 bunch of small green onions
2 bunches of fresh spinach
1 tbsp. bacon grease

Wash the spinach and always make sure there are no bugs or stones in it until the water runs clear. Trim and remove outer layer of green onions. Rinse to remove all grits. Drizzle bacon grease into a skillet until the pan is hot. Slice green onion tops and bottoms and sauté in hot grease for 1 minute. Add the spinach. If all the spinach does not fit in the pan at once, just cover for a minute, stir, and add more. When all the spinach has wilted some, turn off the heat. Stir the spinach and onions and remove from heat. The spinach will continue to cook for a few minutes even though it is off the heat. It should still be bright green, and that is good. Stir and serve.

Red Beans and Rice

When I was living with my daughter in Allentown, Pennsylvania, I wanted beans and rice. However, if I had no time to cook, I would make pork and beans with instant rice. We had Jiffy mix for corn bread. It was nowhere near as good. We ate it after improvising it up a little with green onions and a side of sliced tomatoes. With this recipe, you can use red, pinto, white, or dry black-eyed peas with equal results.

1/2 bag of dry red beans
2 ham hocks
1 sliced salt pork
1 onion
1/2 stalk of celery
1 tbsp. grease rendered from salt pork
1 dry red pepper
1/2 tsp. salt
1 bay leaf

Wash the beans thoroughly and soak them overnight, if you have time. Boil the beans in a saucepan. When the pot comes to a boil, turn off the heat and cover. Let it soak at least 2 hours. Meanwhile, boil the ham hocks in half-filled pot on medium heat. It should cook slowly and simmer while the beans are soaking.

Drain the beans and add to pot with the ham hocks along with the onion and celery. Add some grease, red pepper, and salt. Then boil on medium heat for 2 hours while covered. Stir often to avoid sticking. Do not cook the meat with the beans until it falls apart because some bones will be in the beans. Instead, when the bones are tender enough, take the meat out of the pot and let the beans continue to cook until tender. Uncover the pot and mash some of the beans against the pot. Stir the beans and continue to boil, mashing the beans every 20 minutes until all the beans are done. Cook a pot of rice to pour the beans on. Sprinkle with green onions and serve with hot corn bread.

Sautéed Squash, Cabbage, and Zucchini

1 small yellow squash
1 zucchini
1/4 of small cabbage
1/2 sweet onion, thinly sliced
1 green onion
1/2 tsp. salt
1 tbsp. sugar
1 tbsp. bacon grease
2 slices bacon or 1 thinly slice salt pork (optional)
1/4 tsp. crushed red pepper
zest of 1 lemon

Julienne the squash and zucchini into strips. Finely slice a small wedge of fresh green cabbage, preferably flat head if you can find it. You can also use celery cabbage or Chinese cabbage, but not the hard bottom half. In a medium skillet, slowly fry 2 slices of bacon or salt pork until rendered (all the fat is cooked out and bacon is crisp). Remove bacon. Use the bacon grease to fry the onion, squash, and zucchini over medium heat. Add lemon zest and crushed red pepper, stirring constantly. Add thinly sliced green onion (white and green parts) along with cabbage. Cover. Continue to cook, stirring constantly for 2 minutes until cabbage is wilted. Add sea salt and sugar. Stir and remove from heat. As all vegetables do, this will continue to cook while cooling. It is important that you do not overcook or leave unattended. Dish should be crisp tender. If you want them softer, cover and let it steam, but do not continue to cook.

Stewed Tomatoes

3 or 4 large fresh tomatoes
1/2 c. sugar
1/2 tsp. salt
1/2 tsp. black pepper
1/4 c. water
1/4 c. apple cider vinegar (optional)

Wash, peel, and cut the tomatoes into bite-size pieces. Tomatoes will naturally produce more liquid. Combine tomatoes with all ingredients and simmer for at least an hour. This will create a thick sauce and coat the back of a spoon. If you like it a little sweeter, add a touch more sugar. Adjust seasoning.

Place in serving bowls and put buttered croutons on top.

Tobacco Onion Rings

1 sweet or white onion sliced
1/2 c. flour
1 tsp. salt
1/2 tsp. red or cayenne pepper
1 tsp. cornstarch

Soak sliced onion rings in salted water for at least 15 minutes. Drain. Shake in a plastic bag with all other ingredients. Fry in hot oil until crisp.

Turnip Greens

2 bunches of turnip green or 1 bunch of turnips and 1 bunch of mustards
3 tbsp. lard
3 tbsp. baking soda
3 tbsp. bacon or salt pork grease
3 tbsp. sugar

When you buy fresh greens, always try to get a bright green selection with no brown spots and not too many wormholes. Some holes are unavoidable. Pick and wash turnip greens thoroughly until all grit is out. After washing, break greens up and soak in water with 3 heaping tablespoons of baking soda. Let the greens sit about 5 minutes in soda water.

Render 1 or 2 pieces of salt pork or bacon in pot large enough to hold the greens. After the meat is cooked, add some red pepper and the drained greens a handful at a time. Stir well. When all the greens have been added, sprinkle 2 tablespoons of sugar and 3 tablespoons of lard. Keep stirring. Then add a cup at a time of the ham hock juice. Greens will produce more water so do not add a lot. Feel your way a little at a time. (*Read the art of using just enough.*) The greens should wilt down some before adding hot liquid. Cook for about 10 minutes. Taste for desired doneness. Greens will get tender based on its freshness and the length of the soda soak.

I only cook my greens about 10–15 minutes. Remember that they will continue to cook in a hot pot. If the greens are old, they might need a few more minutes.

White Beans (Dry)

1/2 bag of dry white navy beans
2 ham hocks
1 onion
1/2 stalk celery
1 tbsp. bacon grease
1 dry red pepper
1/2 tsp. salt
1 bay leaf

Pick through beans to remove any rocks or beans that should be discarded. Wash and soak the beans overnight if you have time. Put the beans in the saucepan with 3 inches of water and heat it. When the pot comes to a boil, turn off the heat and cover the saucepan. Let it soak at least 2 hours. Meanwhile, boil ham hocks in a pot filled halfway with water on medium heat in a slow but steady boil.

Drain the beans and add to the pot with the ham hocks along with chopped onions and celery. Add grease (you can use the bacon grease), red pepper, bay leaf, and salt. Continue to boil covered on medium heat for 1 1/2 hours. Mash some of the beans against the pot. Continue to boil, mashing the beans every 10 minutes until all are done for another 1/2 hour. Do not cook the meat with the beans until it falls apart because some bones will be in the beans. Instead, when the ham hocks are tender enough, take the meat out of the pot and let the beans continue to cook until tender. Cut the meat and add them back into the beans. Serve with hot corn bread. Sprinkle with green onions and serve with rice.

PASTA SIDES

Mac and Cheese

11/2 c. macaroni
1/2 tsp. salt
1/2 tsp. black pepper
a pinch of nutmeg
1 8 oz. pack mild cheddar
1 8 oz. sharp cheddar
1/2 c. of your favorite mixed cheese

1/2 c. American cheese
1 tbsp. flour
1/2 stick of butter
1 large can of PET milk
1 egg
1/2 c. milk
1/2 c. buttered breadcrumbs

For crumbs, I use the ends of bread or old buns and crumble them when they're cold. It's easier when it comes out of the freezer. Put in pie pan and add some butter. Heat in the oven until butter melts. Coat the crumbs and set aside.

Add macaroni to 5 cups of water with salt. Boil for about 12 to 15 minutes until macaroni is tender. Drain. Butter a casserole dish and set aside. In another saucepan, melt butter and add flour, salt, and pepper. Add 1/2 cup of milk and stir until smooth. Beat the egg and PET milk together, mixing well. Add to the milk and flour mixture. Add the cheddar cheeses. Add the drained macaroni and mix until macaroni is covered in the cheese sauce. Transfer into a casserole dish and sprinkle it with shredded American cheese on top, pressing down. Bake in the oven at 350 degrees F for 15 minutes. Remove from the oven and sprinkle with additional cheese and crumbs. Return to the oven and bake for 15 minutes more.

Spicy Spaghetti

I prefer this as a side dish with pork chops or chicken fried steak.

1 32 oz. jar of marinara sauce
1 small can Ro-Tel Original tomatoes
1/2 tsp. crushed red pepper or 1/4 tsp. cayenne or red pepper
1/2 tsp. salt
1 tbsp. chopped garlic
1/2 small box of cooked thin spaghetti
1/2 c. chopped green pepper
2 small stalks of chopped celery
1/2 onion, chopped

2 tbsp. sugar
1 tsp. butter or oil
1 tbsp. Italian seasoning or a combination of basil, oregano, thyme, and cracked rosemary
1 tsp. of hot sauce
1 tbsp. lime juice
1 lb. ground beef chuck (80/20 optional)

Cook the spaghetti according to package directions and drain. Sauté vegetables with garlic and red pepper in butter. Add tomatoes and sauce to the mixture and simmer slowly for 10 minutes. Add hot sauce, lime juice, and salt. Stir. Add sugar and Italian seasoning. Taste and adjust seasonings. Add an additional dash of hot sauce if needed. Mix in spaghetti and combine.

If using meat, brown ground beef in a large skillet and drain. If you do not have a lot of liquid after browning, (depends on how fatty your beef is), you can push meat aside and add butter, onion, green pepper, and celery to the skillet, sautéing until just barely tender. Add garlic and crushed red pepper. Stir the meat and vegetables together with seasonings. Drain if desired. Mix and serve on top of spaghetti.

Pasta Filling for Stuffed Shells
from Donnis Eitson

2 pints of small curd cottage cheese
1 1/2 c. shredded mozzarella
1/2 c. shredded Parmesan cheese
1 tsp. crushed basil
1 tsp. oregano
1 tsp. parsley
1 or 2 beaten eggs

Empty both pints of cottage cheese in a medium mixing bowl with beaten eggs. Mix well until thoroughly blended. Add 1 cup of mozzarella and 1/4 cup of Parmesan cheese. Add seasonings and mix well. Stuff the large pasta shells with the mixture and place in a casserole dish in a single layer. Cover with your favorite pasta sauce and bake for 30 minutes at 350 degrees F. Mix the remaining cheese and sprinkle them on top of your pasta dish ten minutes before it is done. Return to the oven for 10–12 minutes until cheese has melted.

Hint, use no-boil pasta shells for less prep time.

SANDWICHES

Grilled Cheese Dream

4 slices of honey wheat bread
1 thinly sliced tomato
2 slice American cheese
2 slice pepper jack cheese
mayo
butter or margarine

Spread mayo on one side of each slice of bread. Spread margarine on the other side. Brown one side in a griddle pan or skillet. Turn. Add cheese to the grilled side with 1 large slice of tomato. Cover with other slice that has been browned. When the downside is brown. Flip and brown the reverse side.

For a real crazy kick, add a couple of slices of spicy sweet pickle.

Pork Chop Sandwich

boneless pork chops
Vidalia onion, sliced
hamburger buns
butter
mayo

Soak the pork chops in salt water for at least 30 minutes. Rinse and trim the fat as needed, but do not trim all of it. A little fat will add flavor and has a good bite when fried. Season chops with meat tenderizer and black pepper. Beat the meat on both sides to tenderize it. Dust it with flour thoroughly and fry in hot skillet until brown on both sides. Drain on paper towels.

Butter buns on one side and mayo to the other side. Grill until brown on both sides. Sauté some onions until tender and add to each pork chop sandwich. Add condiments per preference.

Hamburger

When I was in my tweens, we went down South every summer, usually during the Fourth of July holiday. Most of the parents worked in factories that closed for two weeks during the heat of summer up north, so everyone went back home then. Most of my mama's family lived in or near Bruce, Mississippi. At that time, we did not go to restaurants or stop by the wayside for food. We always had a box lunch. We had not heard of hamburger parlors that we could afford to go to. In Bruce, my mama's Couzin Lucille was where we went to eat. She had a juke joint. How exciting! It was the place everybody went to listen to music and eat. Well, Lucille made burgers that were awesome. They were simple with lots of fried onions. It had no equal. I still prefer simple, not-too-thick hamburgers with lots of fried and raw onions on a grilled bun.

1 lb. 80/20 ground chuck steak	mayo
1 tbsp. Worchester sauce	butter
1 tsp. sea salt	brioche buns
1/2 tsp. black pepper	slices of pepper jack cheese if desired
1 sweet onion sliced	

Mix 80/20 ground chuck with Worchester sauce, steak sauce, salt, and pepper. Form into 1/2 inch patties. Split buns. Butter one side of bun and spread mayo on the other side. Brown each side and put aside. Add sliced onion to skillet and cook until almost translucent. Push to side of skillet and add patties two at a time. Do not crowd skillet. Use a paper towel to absorb some of the liquid. Flatten with a spatula. Cook until brown on one side and flip. When you turn each patty, add a slice or two of cheese and put some of the browned onions on top of the cheese. Remove from skillet when the other side is brown.

MAIN DISHES

Baked Chicken

1 whole chicken	4 tbsp. flour
3 carrots	1/2 stick of butter
1 onion	multiple blend seasoning (Mrs. Dash)
4 stalks of celery	black pepper
1 can of chicken broth	sea salt

Clean, wash, and chop the vegetables in big chunks. Set aside until ready to add to pan.

Wash and clean inside of the chicken, removing the inner gizzard bag. Submerge the chicken completely with water with 4 or 5 tablespoons of salt. Soak the chicken in salted water for at least a couple of hours. Rinse the chicken, pat dry with paper towels, and put in shallow baking pan.

Season the inside of chicken with herbs, salt, and pepper. Squeeze lemon juice on top of chicken and stuff the inside with a half lemon and a quarter or half an onion. Bind the legs with a string. Lightly pull skin from breast by putting your fingertips between the skin and meat. Insert pats of butter between the skin and meat as far as you can reach without tearing the skin. Tuck the wings under the breast toward the back. Baste the chicken with melted butter and season it all over with herbs, pepper, and sea salt. Let it rest for about an hour, if time permits.

Bake in the oven at 500 degrees F oven for 15 minutes, breast side down. Turn chicken over for 15 minutes. Add carrots, onion, and celery around chicken. Lower the heat to 375 degrees F and cook for another 15 minutes. The meat should be getting lightly browned and the vegetables crisp tender. Add 1 cup of chicken broth to the pan. Lower heat to 350 degrees F and cook until the leg moves freely.

Make roux with flour and enough butter to moisten and brown. Add 1 chicken bouillon cube and mix well. Add enough chicken broth to the mixture, approximately 1 cup to 1 1/2 cups, and mix until smooth. Drizzle on the chicken with vegetables. Cook until bubbly and serve with mashed potatoes or rice. Add a small salad and some crusty bread as desired.

Charcoal-Grilled Chicken

Wash chicken and split down the middle. Soak in salt water for at least 2 hours, covering the chicken completely. Wash chicken again and season on both sides with black pepper and salt, Mrs. Dash, or barbeque seasoning. I use a little of each.

Make a fire on the grill and stack coals to one side. Use a chicken rack, putting half on each side. Put chicken on the opposite side of the fire. Open all holes on grill. Put grill cover on with holes over the chicken. Cook for 1 hour 15 minutes without opening the grill. Check the leg for doneness. Make sure the leg turns easily before removing chicken. If the skin is crisp, the chicken should be done. If not, cook for an additional 10 minutes.

If you do not have a chicken rack, use an inverted rib rack or lay on heavy aluminum foil that you have used a knife to put a few slits in.

Alternately, follow prep directions and spread the hot charcoal. Cook chicken directly on rack over coals, turning often. Watch carefully and baste with a solution of 1/2 vinegar and 1/2 water with a brush until done.

Barbeque Pork Butt

1 pork butt
2 tbsp. vinegar
meat tenderizer

Rinse well. Rub each butt with vinegar on both sides and sprinkle with meat tenderizer. Be sure that butt is wet with vinegar on both sides and then generously season with spices as desired. (I do not season a butt because all the tender meat is inside, and I almost always use sauce.)

If smoking the butt, you want to bank the coals to one side. Make sure to have enough coals for a good smoke. Put butt into a rack or on top of a double-folded aluminum foil and place off the heat on the other side of the fire. Leave all the air holes open to start. Cover the grill with the holes that are directly over the side of the grill with the meat.

Barbeque Ribs and Smoked Sausage

Barbeque Ribs
with Barbeque Sauce

baby back ribs
Kansas City-style ribs
slab ribs
1/4 c. salt
1 c. vinegar
1/4 c. sugar
1/2 c. any combo of spices (like a steak rub)
thyme
meat tenderizer

Depending on the cut of rib you use, follow the directions on the label. All types will use the same instructions after cutting. If a slab is cut across the top at the bone line (joint), it does not need further cutting. This is a Kansas City rib. Baby backs need to be slashed slightly if the ends are thick. Just make little slits, but not all the way to the bone. Regular slabs have a thick fatty top. Starting at the big end, cut straight across the top. The bottom should be all ribs, and the top will make rib tips. You will use all the rib unless there is a lot of fat to trim, depending on your preference. Pull the membrane from the backs of the ribs. Put a finger under the bottom corner of each rib and pull the milky looking skin off. It may not all come off in one piece. That is okay. Just take off all you can. You will get good at this.

Soak ribs in water with the 1/4 cup of salt for at least an hour. Rinse the ribs well, rub each one with vinegar on both sides, and sprinkle with meat tenderizer. Apple cider vinegar is good, but white vinegar yields a better flavor that marries well with the sauce. Now generously season.

If freezing for later use, wrap the ribs on aluminum foil. Foil each rib and stack. Then cover all with foil. If cooking, just stack ribs together after soaking in vinegar and seasoning then cover with plastic wrap up at least 2 hours. I usually season the night before.

Ribs can be grilled or smoked. For grilling, take a large saucepan and combine 1 part water to 1/2 vinegar in a pan. For instance, 2 cups of water to 1 cup of vinegar, depending on the number of ribs. Then add 1 or 2 tablespoons. of red or cayenne pepper. Heat water until just simmering. Take off the heat and use it to baste the ribs. When grilling, use the direct heat method and turn ribs often, basting after each turn.

When golden brown, push fire to one side of the grill. Stack the ribs onto aluminum foil, add a little basting liquid, and close tightly. Let it sit on grill off heat until tender. If smoking the ribs, you want to bank the coals to one side. Make sure to have enough coals for a good smoke. Put the ribs into a rack and place off the heat on the other side of the fire. Leave all the air holes open to start. Cover the grill so that the holes are directly over the side of the grill with the meat.

Barbeque Sauce

My sauce, which everyone thinks is awesome, is made up of some of my favorite condiments. Mix, follow directions, and enjoy it.

2 16 oz. bottles of Open Pit original barbeque sauce
1 10 oz. bottle of Heinz 57 sauce
1 10 oz. bottle of A1 Steak Sauce
1/2 c. yellow mustard
1 c. ketchup
1/4 c. Worchester sauce
1/2 12 oz. jar of orange marmalade
1/4 c. Frank's hot sauce
1 tbsp. Tabasco

Mix all ingredients in a large saucepan. Simmer over low heat for about 1 hour, stirring frequently.

Baked Bacon

1 lb. bacon, preferably fatter then lean

In a rimmed jelly roll pan or a cookie sheet pan, spread the bacon out in single slices side by side. Preheat the oven at 350 degrees F. You can add the bacon as soon as you turn on the oven. The bacon will cook as the oven heats. Turn bacon often until totally rendered (all the fat is cooked). Drain on paper towels. Serve hot or at room temperature. Reserve the bacon fat for cooking vegetables or soups as a favorable seasoning.

Beef Short Ribs and Potatoes

2 lbs. beef short ribs or beef ribs
5 medium potatoes, cut in chunks
1 onion, diced
3 stalks celery, chopped
1 chicken bouillon cubes
3 beef bouillon cubes
5 tbsp. flour
1 tsp. black pepper
2 tbsp. grease

Soak bones in salted water for at least 1/2 hour then rinse. Heat grease in skillet until hot. Dust the bones and lightly brown each piece. Transfer to a casserole dish or baking pan. Pour 1 1/2 cup of water to the bones and add onion and celery around meat. Add bouillon cubes to pan and bake at 350 degrees F until fork tender. Add potatoes and cook until potatoes are fork tender.

Take 3 tablespoons of flour and mix with water to just make a paste. Stir until smooth. Add a little of the broth from meat and then add back into a pan with the meat. Cook for an additional 15 minutes until it becomes thickened. You can also boil in a gallon pot. After browning, add the bones and vegetables to pot with water and simmer on low heat. Add potatoes when almost done.

Beef Rump Roast

1 beef roast
3 slice bacon
3 tbsp. oil
1/4 onion, diced
1/2 c. flour
4 medium potatoes
1/2 onion, sliced
4 carrots
2 stalks celery, sliced into 1/2 pieces
1 beef bouillon cube
black pepper
meat tenderizer

Wash the beef roast. Season with pepper and sprinkle meat tenderizer all over. Heat oil in oven-safe Dutch oven pot until hot. Add the roast and brown on each side. Lay strips of bacon across the roast while in the pot. Sprinkle the diced onion around the roast and bake in a 350 oven for 1 to 1 1/2 hours. Add the chopped celery to the pot. Mix the bouillon cube with a 1/2 cup of water. If the roast is large and not quite knife tender, bake for another 1/2 hour. However, you don't want it falling apart at this point. Remove the roast.

Meanwhile, peel and cut potatoes into quarters. Peel carrots and cut into serving-size pieces. Cut a large onion into slices and add vegetables into the pot. Return to the oven and let it cook while you make the gravy. Melt 2 tablespoons of butter in a skillet and add 1/4 cup of flour. Brown flour a little. Add some of the juice from the roast to the skillet. Stir until smooth. If needed, add additional water to make a smooth gravy.

Slice the roast with a sharp knife. Place the slices close together on top of the vegetables. Cover with the gravy and return it to the oven. Cook for 15 minutes or until meat is tender. A beef roast is easier to slice when it is just tender with a sharp knife. Do not slice if juices are still red. Cook a little longer first.

Boiled Neck Bones

When I was a little girl in elementary school, my grandmother Hellon used to fix my lunch for school. I remember so vividly the day she wrapped up a neck bone and a piece of wonder bread. I know it was wonder bread because that was the only bread everybody bought. There is not much meat on any neck bone to start with, so it was not the most filling lunch one could have. The strange thing is that I did not know enough to question the lunch or be embarrassed by it. Innocence and youth has its rewards. My grandma was so proud to be able to give me lunch. Imagine that!

fresh neck bones
1 stalk celery
1/2 onion
red pepper
salt and pepper to taste

Wash the neck bones and parboil. To parboil, cover meat with water. When the water starts to boil, turn off the heat and drain. It is best to pour the water and bones into a clean sink. Trim the bones of excess fat and membrane. Wash the bones again and also the scum from the pot the bones were parboiled in. Fill the pot with fresh water. Add a stalk of celery, 1/2 onion, salt, and black pepper. I also add a piece of dried red pepper to the pot. Cook until bones are tender but not falling apart for 1 1/2 to 2 hours.

Neck Bones with Beans

Follow the cooking directions for neck bones above.

Add presoaked dried beans, (pinto, red, or white beans) to the pot after parboiling and rewashing the bones. If you want to cook the beans with the bones, then it is best to chop the celery and the onion. Reduce the red pepper pod by half. When the beans are almost done in about 1 1/2 hours, use a fork to mash some of the beans in the pot to thicken the liquid. Continue to cook until meat and beans are tender. It will require about 1/2 hour additional cooking time.

Do not cook the meat with the beans until it falls apart because some bones will be in the beans. Instead, when the bones are tender enough, take them out of pot and let the beans continue to cook until tender. Serve meat and beans together. Hot corn bread and rice are perfect for this dish.

Chicken Fried Pork or Beef Cube Steaks

3 or 4 cubed pork or beef steaks
1 egg
1/2 c. milk
1 c. flour
1/2 tsp. baking powder
1 tsp. meat tenderizer
1 tsp. black pepper
1 c. oil to fry

Rinse cube steaks lightly. Be careful not to tear them apart. Cut out any tough membrane if visible with a sharp knife.

Mix flour, black pepper, and baking powder in a shallow dish or a plate. Lightly beat 1 egg until well mixed and add milk. Heat some oil in a skillet until a pinch of flour sizzles. Dip beef cubes in egg mixture and then into the separate bowl with the flour. Carefully place the steaks to the skillet without crowding. Turn when they brown on one side. Be sure to move steaks around hot skillet a little after turning so they do not stick. When all sides are nicely browned, remove from skillet and drain on paper towels. Be sure to bring oil back to frying temperature before adding more steaks.

If desired, sauté some onions until done to garnish the cube steaks.

Corned Beef and Cabbage

1 med. cabbage
corned beef
packet of seasoning
2 tbsp. brown sugar

Do not rinse the corned beef. Add corned beef and the juice from the package into a pot and fill it with enough water to submerge it. Add the seasoning packet included in the corned beef. Boil until tender for 2 1/2 to 3 hours.

Wash and cut cabbage into chunks. Soak in water with 2 heaping tablespoons of baking soda for 3 to 5 minutes. Drain. Remove corned beef from the cooking liquid. Boil liquid rapidly to reduce to about 2 cups. Drain. Add drained liquid back into pot and bring to a boil. Add cabbage along with a little sugar. Boil for about 5 minutes until tender. Remove from heat.

If desired, put corned beef on an aluminum covered cookie sheet and sprinkle with brown sugar. Bake until the brown sugar melts and make a glaze. Slice corned beef against the grain and serve on top of the cabbage.

The brine is important. This chicken will not be salty or sweet from the brine.

Fried Chicken (Brined)

You may use assorted pieces of chicken with wings sectioned and breast cut into at least 2 pieces. Wash chicken and singe wings and drumsticks. Dissolve 1/2 cup of salt and 1/4 cup of sugar in water. Soak for a minimum of a couple of hours.

2 1/2 c. flour
1 tsp. black pepper
1/2 tsp. salt
2 tbsp. cayenne
1/2 c. hot sauce
1 c. buttermilk
1/2 tsp. poultry seasoning

To brine

Wash chicken after the brine and pat dry. Season with cayenne and cover chicken completely with hot sauce and buttermilk. At this point, you can leave the chicken in the buttermilk soak for up to 8 hours in the refrigerator if you have time. When you are ready to fry, take it out of refrigerator, stir, and let sit for at least an hour at room temperature.

To fry

Always have chicken close to room temperature before frying; otherwise, it will lower the temperature of the oil too much and your fried chicken will be soggy. Put 2 1/2 to 3 cups of flour in a plastic bag. Add 1 tablespoon cayenne, 1/2 teaspoon salt, 1 teaspoon black pepper, and 1/2 to 1 teaspoon poultry seasoning. Shake to mix. Add chicken pieces a few at a time to cover well.

Meanwhile, pour canola cooking oil to a skillet up to at least 2 inches. Heat the oil to 350 degrees F. To gauge the temperature, use a candy thermometer or sprinkle a pinch of flour in a skillet. Flour should immediately sizzle. If not, let oil heat a little more. If the oil is not hot enough, the flour will not adhere and the chicken will be oily. Add chicken but don't crowd them. Cover immediately. Fry until lightly browned on one side and then turn the chicken. After both sides are brown, lower the heat slightly until done. Remove the lid after you have lightly browned both sides.

Bring the oil back to 350 degrees F if you have additional pieces to fry. If necessary, strain oil into a heatproof container and add back into the skillet. Always add to hot oil to keep a crust. If your flour does not make a crust, it means your oil is not hot enough.

Without buttermilk

If you do not have buttermilk or do not like the taste, simply use hot sauce. The chicken will be just as good and will not be too hot. I usually use an entire small 6 oz. bottle plus cayenne pepper to soak before cooking.

Fried Catfish

catfish fillets
1/2 c. flour
3/4 c. cornmeal
1/2 tsp. salt
1/4 tsp. cayenne pepper
1/2 tsp. pepper
1/2 c. buttermilk
oil for frying

Wash and pat the fillets dry. Cut into 3-inch strips if you want a crispier fish, instead of a thicker steak-like piece. Soak in buttermilk for at least 1/2 hour. Drain and season with salt and pepper. Mix in flour and meal with cayenne pepper. Coat the fillets with the meal mixture. Heat the oil to 360 degrees F. Fry in hot oil until golden brown and crispy, about 5 minutes per side. If you cut the fillets in strips for fingers, the frying time will be less. Drain on paper towels and serve hot.

Fried Chicken Strip Sandwich

Fried Chicken Strips

2 large chicken beasts
1/4 c. salt
1/2 c. hot sauce
1 c. buttermilk
1 1/2 c. flour
1 tsp. cayenne pepper
1/2 tsp. black pepper
1/4 tsp. poultry seasoning
pinch of salt
water

Trim the skin and membrane from the chicken and cut into strips of 1/2 inch thick. Soak breasts in salted water for at least an hour. Rinse and dry with paper towels as well as you can. Add the strips to a mix of hot sauce and buttermilk in a pot or ziplock bag. Let it stand in buttermilk for at least an hour or two. Mix flour with the rest of the seasonings into a plastic bag. Add chicken strips a few at a time and shake well to coat well.

Heat 2 cups of oil until 350 degrees F. Make sure the oil is hot. If you do not have a thermometer, pinch a little flour in the oil. It should sizzle immediately. If not, heat a little more. Add chicken slowly and do not crowd. Cook until golden brown. You should not have to turn the strips too often because they are small and will be covered in the hot oil, but do turn as needed.

Fried Pork Chops

When I made dinner for my husband the first time, I wanted to keep it simple and quick. I decided on fresh fried corn and fried pork chops along with some sliced tomatoes. I cannot tell you from that day to this one if my husband was savoring the look of the chops on the table or the one in the chair (me).

4 1/2 thick pork chops or 6 thin pork slices
1 tsp. meat tenderizer
1 tsp. black pepper
1 c. self-rising flour or 1 c. flour mixed with 1/2 tsp. baking powder
1 c. vegetable oil or Crisco

Soak pork chops in salt water for at least 30 minutes. Rinse and trim the fat as needed. Season chops with meat tenderizer and black pepper. Tenderize the meat on both sides with a blunt edge of a knife or a mallet. Flour thoroughly. Heat oil in a cast-iron skillet until a little pinch of flour sizzles when you sprinkle it in the oil. Turn the pork chops around so they do not stick in the skillet. When brown on one side in about 3 minutes, turn again and lower the heat slightly. Brown both sides, turning at least twice.

I like a crispy pork chop. Drain excess oil on paper towels for a few minutes. Then place them on a serving platter.

Oxtail Stew

A favorite recipe of Martha

2 ears of fresh corn cut off the cob or 1/2 tube of frozen cream corn
4 fresh tomatoes or 2 14.5 oz. cans of Petite Diced tomatoes (best combo is 3 fresh tomatoes and 1 can of Petite Diced)
1 can Ro-Tel Original diced tomatoes
1 onion, diced
3 beef bouillon cubes
2 chicken cubes
1 1/2 lbs. oxtails, parboiled and washed
1 medium potato, diced
3 tbsp. sugar
1/4 small head of cabbage, shredded.
1/2 dozen spaghetti sticks
okra (if desired)

Parboil oxtails and drain. Then add in fresh water after washing the oxtails. Start the pot boiling again into a good constant boil, but not rolling. Add the bouillon cubes to the pot and continue boiling for approximately 1 1/2 hours. By this time, they should be getting tender. Add the chopped onion and continue to boil for another 1/2 hour. The liquid should be now reduced by half. Add tomatoes. Use one can of Ro-Tel Mild or hot tomatoes for extra seasoning and heat. If you have fresh tomatoes, it is okay to use them instead of using canned. Bring back to a boil.

The oxtails should now be tender. Add cabbage, potatoes, sugar, and corn. Cook for 15 minutes. Mix 1/4 cup of flour or 2 tablespoons of cornstarch with 1/4 cup of water. Mix until smooth. Get a couple spoons of liquid from the pot and mix with flour water. Add to pot along with spaghetti. Stir frequently to avoid sticking.

Serve with corn bread.

Braised Ox Tails, Potatoes and Spinach

Braised Ox Tails

2 lbs. ox tails
1 onion diced
3 stalks celery sliced
1 chicken bouillon cube
1 beef bouillon cube
½ c. flour
1 tsp. black pepper
2 tbsp. grease or oil

Rinse bones in salted water. Heat grease or oil in skillet until hot. Flour ox tails and lightly brown each piece. Remove to covered casserole dish or baking pan as you brown each piece. Add 1 ½ c water and shatter onion and celery around meat. Add bouillon cubes to pan and sprinkle with black pepper. Bake at 250 F until fork tender, about 3 hours.

Take 3 tbsp flour and add enough water to just make a paste. Add a little of the broth from meat stirring until smooth, and then add the smooth roux back into pan with meat. Cook an additional 15 minutes until it becomes thickened.

You can also boil in a stock pot. After browning, add bones, bouillon cubes and vegetables to the pot and cover with water. Simmer on low heat until tender.

Add potatoes and carrots when almost done if desired.

Ribs, Sausage and Kraut

1 bag refrigerated sauerkraut
3 tbsp. brown sugar
4 medium fresh hocks or 1 baby back rib cut into serving-size pieces
1/2 large onion
2 tsp. bacon grease
1 smoked sausage (optional)

Boiling method (Using shanks)

Wash the kraut, drain, and set aside. Parboil some shanks. Rinse and return to a clean pot with enough water to cover the hocks. Season with salt and pepper. Cook for 1 hour in a slow boil. Add kraut, onion, and bacon grease. Continue to cook until the hocks are fork tender. Add brown sugar after the water has almost evaporated. Stir and enjoy.

Oven method (Using ribs)

If cooking kraut and sausage or ribs, bake ribs in the oven at 375 degrees F for about 45 minutes until lightly browned. Lower the temperature to 350 degrees F. Add sausage and cook until sausage is lightly browned (about 15 minutes). Leave about 2 teaspoon of grease from meat in pan. Cover the ribs and sausage with the rinsed kraut and sprinkle with chopped onion, brown sugar, and crushed red pepper if desired. Cover tightly and continue to bake in the oven for another hour until meat is fork tender.

Quick Pork Chop Suey

1 lb. pork tenderloin
1/2 tsp. red pepper flakes
1 can bean sprouts
1 large onion
4 large stalks of celery
1 beef bouillon cube
1 chicken bouillon cube
1/4 c. soy sauce
1/2 Chinese cabbage wedge, shredded

1 8 oz. can bamboo shoots,
   drained (optional)
1/4 c. flour or cornstarch
1/4 red bell pepper, cut in
   thin strips (optional)
1/2 c. mushrooms
2 green onions
1 can beef gravy
meat tenderizer
black pepper

Skin membrane from pork tenderloin. Cut down the middle of each section (usually comes as a two piece, but I only use one section). Then slice into bite-size pieces. Slice celery diagonally into 1/4 inch slices. Cut medium onion in half and lay cut side down to slice thinly. Remove seeds and core from red pepper. Lightly sauté the vegetables in to pot for 2 minutes. Remove with a slotted spoon.

In a large Dutch oven, brown sliced pork in 1 tablespoon of oil. Rinse bean sprouts in colander. Add bean sprouts, bamboo shoots, and mushrooms to the pot. Cook for 2 minutes, stirring frequently. Add beef and chicken bouillon cubes to the pot, mashing the cubes into liquid formed in pan. Push vegetables to one side. Add flour and cornstarch to 1/4 cup of water to make a paste. Stir into pot. Add cabbage and gravy and stir. Bring to a boil and let simmer 10 minutes. Add a little water if necessary. Add soy sauce and red pepper. Serve over hot rice. Sprinkle with chow mein noodles if desired.

Quick Steak Marinade

rib eye or strip steak
1 tbsp. Worchester sauce
2 tbsp. chopped garlic
1 tbsp. A1 sauce
1/2 freshly squeezed lemon
2 tbsp. balsamic vinegar
meat tenderizer
1/2 tsp. sea salt
1 tsp. pepper

Wash meat and trim if needed. Do not remove all the fat. It adds tenderness and flavor. Sprinkle both sides of meat with tenderizer, sea salt, and black pepper. Mix all other ingredients together and pour over meat. Cover well with marinade. Flip steak for every 15 minutes for at least an hour. Cook as desired. If grilling, be sure grill is hot and spray with cooking spray before adding meat. If cooking in oven, heat skillet until extremely hot. Add 2 tablespoons of butter. It should sizzle quickly. Add steaks. Brown on one side flip and put under the broiler until the other side is brown.

Roast Turkey
with Cornbread Dressing and Giblet Gravy

1 midsize turkey (9–12 lbs.)
2 cartons or 4 cans of chicken broth
2 stalks of celery
1/2 onion
1 stick of butter
Sea salt
Pepper

For a smaller turkey and I prefer Butterball.

Thaw the turkey if frozen. Wash and clean inside of turkey as well as possible, removing the inner gizzard bag. Submerge the turkey completely in water and add with at least 1/2 cup of salt. Soak the turkey in salted water a couple of hours or overnight in a refrigerator. Rinse thoroughly inside and out. Put in a roaster pan that is large enough and heavy enough to hold the bird.

Season the inside and outside of turkey with salt and pepper. Squeeze half a lemon on top of the turkey and stuff a couple stalks of celery and some onion inside it. Truss legs with sting. Lightly pull skin from breast by putting your fingertips between the skin and meat. Insert pats of butter between the skin and meat as far as you can reach without tearing the skin. Tuck the wings under the breast toward the back. Baste the turkey with melted butter and season all over with pepper and sea salt. Let it rest for about an hour, if time permits. Bake in the oven at 500 degrees F for 15 minutes, breast side down. Turn turkey over for 15 minutes.

Lower the oven to 400 degrees F and cook for another 15 minutes. The bird should be getting lightly browned. Add 1 carton or 2 cans of chicken broth to the pan. Cover the pan with a lid or heavy aluminum foil.

Lower the heat to 350 degrees F and cook until leg moves freely, and the turkey is golden brown. Add 2 chicken bouillon cubes to the broth and use the broth for the dressing and gravy.

Dressing

9-inch skillet with homemade corn bread
1 1/2 c. stuffing cubes
1 c. onion, diced
1 c. celery, chopped
1 c. green pepper, diced
1/2 tbsp. poultry seasoning
2 eggs, well beaten
2 slices toasted bread
1 stick of butter
1 6 oz. Stovetop Chicken Stuffing Mix
1 cup cooked giblets (cooked until tender and chopped)
Chicken broth from the turkey
Sage rubbed (fresh rubbed is best) to taste
1 carton of chicken broth (additional)

Make a pan of corn bread with egg. Homemade; not Jiffy. Do not let it get real brown. Finely chop 1 to 1 1/2 green pepper, 1 large onion, and about 4 stalks of celery to make at least a full cup. Sauté in a stick of butter until soft but not brown. Toast 2 pieces of sandwich bread (any), and set aside to cool. In a large bowl or a dish pan, add cornbread, crumble toast, and stuffing mix. Add sautéed vegetables with the butter and half the giblets. Start with a tablespoon of sage. Pour some chicken broth from the turkey into the stuffing mix. Mix well. Make sure you add broth until this is very moist (canned broth is okay). Check the seasonings. Add sage and 1/2 teaspoon of poultry seasoning. Check the seasoning again. When it needs a little more, stop. It is the little more that becomes too much. Add broth until moist, not runny or soupy. Beat 2 large eggs—or 3, if you have a large dishpan. Add a little broth to the eggs and beat well. Add to the corn bread mixture and then pour into a buttered pan or glass dish. Bake at 325 degrees F until lightly brown. Do not burn it. If needed, bake and then broil a few minutes to brown the top.

Mix and bake until the edges are brown. The center will still be very soft, but it will set as it cools.

Turkey Gravy

Add flour to melted butter and stir until well combined. The flour will absorb the butter but will still be a little loose. You do not want it to be stiff. Add a little chopped onion, maybe 3 tablespoons. Add chicken or turkey broth, stirring constantly until smooth. Adjust the broth for desired thickness. Add the leftover giblets from the dressing. This is the last thing you will cook. You want it hot and still pourable. The gravy will stiffen as it cools.

Giblets

Cut the fat and impurities from the giblets and parboil. Replace the water and boil the giblets again. Add salt and pepper and cook until fork tender for about 1 1/2 hours. Cool and chop. Add the giblets to the dressing and save some for the gravy.

Martha's Pork Chops with Hot Rice

2 large fresh tomatoes or 1 14.5 oz. can of Petite Dice
1 can Ro-Tel spicy tomatoes
1/2 c. coarsely chopped green pepper
1/2 c. coarsely chopped celery
1 medium onion, chopped
2 tsp. hot sauce
1 c. uncooked rice
4 or 5 pork chops
1 c. flour
1 tsp. sugar
1 tsp. salt
meat tenderizer
black pepper

Use a skillet or frying pan with about a 12 inch width with lid or something large enough to hold 4 pork chops.

Trim and rinse the pork chops. Use the blunt end of a knife, heavy spoon, or mallet to lightly pound the chops on both sides. Sprinkle with meat tenderizer and pepper and cover with flour on both sides. Fry the pork chops until browned on both sides. Remove from the skillet. Fry in batches if necessary not to crowd the pan.

Leave some grease from the skillet. Toss in the green pepper, onion, and celery and sauté until soft. Add rice, salt, and sugar. Stir well, coating the rice with oil in the skillet. Add the tomatoes and hot sauce. Pour in a cup of water and stir well. Cook until the mixture starts to boil. It should take about 5 minutes. Lower the heat and lay pork chops on top of the cooking rice. Cover and simmer until rice is done and mixture has absorbed liquid, approximately 30 minutes. Let it cool for a few minutes before serving. The pork chops will be fork tender and rice fluffy.

Baked Ham with Honey and Brown Sugar Glaze

Kentucky boneless ham, shank, or butt half ham
whole cloves
1 1/2 cup brown sugar
1 can of Coca-Cola (not Diet)
1/2 cup honey
1 tbsp. cinnamon
1 tsp. nutmeg

Soak the ham for at least an hour in salt water. I prefer the boneless Kentucky Legend ham. Stick in whole cloves all over the ham, top and bottom. Put in enough cloves to cover every couple of inches. Make grid pattern into squares and use as a guide (I use a lot.).

Put in a baking pan. Pour 1/2 can of Coke over the ham. (You can also use 7 Up, but it does not make a dark syrup like Coke does.) Sprinkle with cinnamon and nutmeg and cover with aluminum foil. Bake slowly at 325 degrees F for 1 to 11/2 hours, depending on size. Remove from oven. Sprinkle brown sugar and more cinnamon on top of the ham then drizzle honey on top of the brown sugar. Make sure the honey is cold so it does not slide off. Put pineapple slices on top with toothpicks, if desired. Put it back in the oven to cook uncovered for an hour. Check often that it does not dry or burn. Add more brown sugar if needed for a honey-baked crust.

- *Tip.* After you serve that ham a few times for dinner or sandwiches, that bone will turn a pot of beans into pure goodness. Wash the beans (white, pinto, red, or lima). If you just want some pea soup, use dried green peas (unsoaked). Soak beans per package directions. Add water to cover the ham bone. Add the beans plus some onion and a little red pepper pod and cook until beans are tender. Dice the ham and skin into the beans, if desired.

Salmon Patties

1 7 oz. can of salmon (Sam's Club is the best.)
1 large egg, well beaten
1/2 small onion, chopped
2 tbsp. flour
3 tbsp. meal
1/4 tsp. salt
1/2 tsp. black pepper

Remove any skin or bones from the salmon. Do not drain. Flake salmon. Beat the egg in a separate bowl and add to salmon along with remaining ingredients, mixing until combined. Fry a heaping spoonful of salmon in a frying pan or skillet. Flatten slightly into a cookie and cook until brown. Then flip and brown the other side. Serve with hot biscuits and jelly.

Glazed Salmon and Green Salad

Salmon Fillet with Glaze

2 1-inch salmon fillets
1/2 tsp. salt
1/2 tsp. black pepper
2 tbsp. brown sugar
3 tbsp. honey
4 pats of butter

Rinse fillets. Season with salt and pepper on both sides. Preheat broiler to low broil. Put salmon on a foil-lined cookie sheet or a 9 x 13 baking pan. Put 1 pat of butter on one side and sprinkle lightly with brown sugar and a little honey. Place under low broiler for approximately 5 minutes. Be careful to have pan a few inches from heat source so it does not burn. Remove from oven. Using a spatula, flip the salmon. Put 1 pat of butter on the other side and sprinkle with brown sugar. Broil for 4 minutes. Remove from oven and cover with the remaining honey. Broil for 2 more minutes. The sugar and honey will make a glaze. Salmon should be lightly browned and flake easily with a fork. It will cook another minute as it sits in the glaze.

Shrimp Creole

This dish is a little spicy with a touch of sweetness. It is thick sauce with vegetables. Try to cut the vegetables into the same size so they will all crisp evenly. I like a sweet onion or white onion instead of a yellow onion, but you can use either. I always add chicken wings to the pot a minute before adding the shrimp because I love the flavor it coats the chicken in, but it is also still crispy. You can, of course, skip the chicken, but then you do not get the combination of flavors.

2 lbs. extra-large shrimp (cleaned and deveined)

3 slices bacon

1 small can of Ro-Tel Original tomatoes

1 can water (use the Ro-Tel can)

1 14.5 oz. can Petite Dice tomatoes or
  2 large fresh tomatoes chopped or
  1 large can of Petite Dice tomatoes

1 bay leaf

2 tbsp. flour

1 tbsp. hot sauce

leftover fried chicken wings (if you have some)

1 tsp. cracked pepper

1 large green pepper, cut into strips

1 large red pepper, cut into strips

1 large yellow pepper, cut into strips

1 large onion, cut into strips

3 stalks of fresh celery, sliced

2 tbsp. sugar

1 tbsp. parsley

1 tbsp. mixed spice (Mrs. Dash)

Boil the shrimps until just pink and rinse. If using frozen shrimp, thaw, rinse, and set aside. In large pot, add the tomatoes, bay leaf, spices, salt, sugar, cracked pepper, and parsley. Simmer for about 1/2 hour until flavors have melded.

Then cut the peppers into strips. (I cut my strips into 1/4-inch strips diagonally. If the peppers are large, I sometimes cut them in half.) Peel a large sweet onion. Cut in half then slice each half into strips. Chop celery into chunks. Fry bacon slowly until you have rendered the fat and the bacon is crisp. Set bacon aside, leaving the grease in the skillet. Add vegetables to the skillet and sauté for 3 or 4 minutes. They should still be crisp tender. Taste the tomatoes and adjust seasonings. Add hot sauce and crumbled bacon to the pot. Mix flour with enough water to make a smooth paste. Add to tomato mixture, stirring constantly until the sauce begins to thicken. Add vegetables to tomatoes and stir. Add shrimp immediately and stir for about 3 minutes until shrimp is done. Serve with hot rice.

Smothered Chicken

1 whole chicken cut up or 8 pcs. of chicken parts
1 c. flour
1 tsp. pepper
1/2 tsp. salt
1/2 onion
1 c. canola oil

Wash the chicken pieces and soak in brine for at least an hour. The bine solution should be 1/2 cup salt to 2 cups of water. Rinse the chicken and season with salt and pepper. Heat oil to at least 350 degrees F. Oil must be hot enough or the flour will not adhere to chicken and the chicken will be soggy.

Fry chicken in a single layer without crowding. Brown on one side and turn chicken frequently to get an even browning. Drain all but 3 tablespoons of the oil into a heatproof container. Leaving some crumbs from the chicken in the skillet with the oil, sprinkle enough flour into the skillet to make a loose paste. Add 1 chicken bouillon cube. Stir until smooth. Add chopped onion and cook with the flour mixture until golden brown. Gradually add 1/4 cup of water to the flour mixture and stir until smooth. Add another 1/4 cup of water and continue stirring. Add enough water for the gravy to have the consistency of syrup, stirring constantly on a medium simmer. Add a little water at a time to get the thickness you want. Place chicken back into gravy, cover, and simmer slowly for at least 30 minutes until chicken is tender. Serve with rice and hot biscuits.

Stuffed Pork Chops

3 thick pork chops or 6 thin ones
1/2 c. celery
1/2 c. onion
1/4 c. green pepper
1/4 c. creamed corn (optional)
1 box stovetop stuffing mix
2 tbsp. butter
4 apples
2 tbsp. brown sugar
2 tbsp. butter

Preheat oven to 350 degrees F.

If using thick pork chops, cut into the chop from the side to the bone so that you make a pocket. If you are using thin chops, then you will use two per serving. Sauté celery, onion, and green pepper in butter until just crisp. Prepare stovetop per package directions and add the vegetables, including the corn, to the stuffing mix. Stuff pocket or put a thick mound of stuffing between 2 chops and stick toothpicks through them to hold together. Mix 2 peeled and sliced apples and brown sugar together until moist (uncooked). Put apples into the bottom of pan. Lay chops on top of apples and cook uncovered in the oven for 15 minutes. Reduce temperature to 350 degrees F, cover tightly, and cook for an addition 45 minutes. Heap on the leftover stuffing on the side of chops. Peel and slice the other apples. Mix in butter and brown sugar. Sauté lightly until apples are crisp and tender. Do not cook until mushy. Serve with stuffed chops and stuffing.

Smothered Pork Chops

4 pork chops
meat tenderizer
1 c. flour
1 tsp. pepper
1/2 tsp. salt
1 onion
1 c. canola oil

Wash and trim pork chops and soak in water to cover with 1/2 teaspoon of salt. Rinse pork chops and season with salt and pepper. Heat oil to at least 350 degrees F. Oil must be hot enough or the flour will not adhere to pork chops and the coating will be soggy. Add chops in a single layer without crowding. Brown one side and turn to cook the other side. The chops should be turned frequently to get an even browning and the meat is cooked through.

Drain skillet leaving some the crumbs from the chops in the skillet. Add 3 tablespoons of oil back into the skillet along with some flour to make a paste. Add 1 chicken bouillon cube. Stir until smooth. Add chopped onion and cook with the flour mixture until golden brown. Gradually add 1/4 cup of water at a time. Continue to stir to keep it smooth. Add enough water for gravy to be the consistency of syrup. Add another 1/2 cup of water if needed. Place pork chops back into gravy, cover, and simmer for at least 30 minutes.

BREADS

Salmon Patties and 7 Up Bisquits

7 Up Biscuits

2 c. flour
2 tsp. baking powder
1/2 tsp. salt
1/4 tsp. baking soda or 2 c. self-rising flour
1/2 c. sour cream
3/4 cup 7 Up
1/4 cup melted butter

Mix flour with baking powder, salt, and baking soda. (If using self-rising flour, omit baking powder and salt). Add sour cream into flour mix and 7 Up. Use more 7 Up as needed to incorporate all the flour to make a soft, wet dough. Use a piece of wax paper to spread out a little flour. Roll the dough onto floured wax paper. Next, sprinkle the top with a little flour and knead the dough. Melt butter into a 9-inch square pan or two 7-inch pie tins. Cut the biscuits and arrange them in pan on top of melted butter. Bake at 450 degrees F for 12 minutes or until golden brown.

Buttermilk Biscuits

2 c. flour
1 tbsp. butter
1/4 c. Crisco
3 1/2 tsp. baking powder
1/2 tsp. baking soda
1 tsp. salt
1 tsp. sugar
1 c. buttermilk

Add butter and Crisco to dry ingredients until it looks like little balls. Add buttermilk and mix lightly until you can get all the flour mixed in. This will be wet when placed on the wax paper. Gently knead the dough, adding flour as needed until you can cut the dough unto biscuits. Moisten your fingers with buttermilk and smooth a little on top of each biscuit before baking. Place biscuits in pan close together. Gather the scraps to knead and make another biscuit. Bake at 450 degrees F for 11–14 minutes until golden.

Skillet Corn Bread for Dressing

1 1/2 c. white meal
1 c. flour
1 tbsp. baking powder
1 tsp. salt
1 egg
1 c. milk
1/2 c. water
4 tbsp. of Crisco or oil

Mix the dry ingredients in bowl. Add the egg that has been slightly beaten with a little milk and tip them into the remainder of the milk. Add the milk and the water to meal mixture along with 2 tablespoons of oil. Mix thoroughly.

Heat the other 2 tablespoons of oil in a skillet until extremely hot. Pour the bread batter into the skillet and bake in the oven at 450 degrees F until set. Brown slightly if necessary.

Corn Bread

1/2 c, milk
1 1/2 c. yellow or white meal
3/4 c. flour mix
1/2 tsp. salt
1 tbsp. baking powder
3 tbsp. oil or bacon grease melted

I do not use sugar, but if you prefer, add a teaspoon to the batter.

Melt the butter in an iron skillet. Mix the rest of ingredients together and add milk. Add enough water to make bread batter resemble a pancake batter. Mix well. Transfer into hot greased skillet and bake at 450 degrees F for 20 minutes. Lightly brown under the broiler if necessary. Place into plate and serve hot.

Corn Bread with Jalapeño and Corn

My grandson Jarrett loved corn bread and caramel cake. But he would eat corn bread without anything on it at any time. He ate all kinds, hot water, milk, sweet, griddle or johnnycakes, if it was corn bread, he loved them all.

2 ears of corn scraped from the cob or 1 tube of frozen corn
1 jalapeño pepper, finely diced
1 green onion, thinly sliced
1/2 c. diced onion
1 c. buttermilk
1 egg, beaten
3/4 c. yellow meal
1/2 c. flour
1/2 tsp. salt
1 tsp. baking powder
1 tsp. sugar
3 tbsp. butter or bacon grease melted

Melt the butter in an iron skillet. Beat the egg and milk together in a bowl. Mix the rest of ingredients together and add to the milk mixture. Turn into hot skillet and bake at 450 degrees F for 20 minutes. Lightly brown under the broiler if necessary. Place into a plate and serve hot.

Hot Water Corn Bread

This is the same as crackling bread without the rinds, and it is a little easier to master.

Mix dry ingredients and have enough boiling water to cover. Stir constantly. It will be very thick. Add a tablespoon of oil. You should need a little more water from the tap to make it smoother—not boiling, but like loose oatmeal. Blend slightly. Fry in hot oil. Turn when brown on one side.

Hot Water Crackling Corn Bread

1/2 c. crackling or pork rind
1 c. meal
1/4 c. flour
1 tbsp. baking powder
1 tsp. salt
boiling water

Hot water corn bread is delicious but takes getting use to when adding the boiling water. Boiling water will cook the meal fast, so be ready to cool down with room temperature tap water.

Mix meal, flour, baking powder, and salt. Pour in about a cup of boiling water and stir fast. It will look like its foaming. That's okay. Stir in just enough tap water to get the batter to smoothen. It will be thick. Add pork rinds or crackling if you have it. The rinds will thicken the batter more, so add a little more hot water if needed.

Heat your oil until very hot, but not smoking. Add big spoonful of batter into the skillet. Brown fast and turn.

I use plain pork rinds. I love the texture and prefer crackling that is not too hard.

JAMS AND JELLIES

Apple Jelly

5 lbs. bag of apples, preferably Granny Smith
sugar
water

Wash apples and cut into quarters without peeling. Then cut the quarters into smaller pieces. Place apples inside a pot and add one inch of water. Boil and simmer until the apples are very soft. Let it sit overnight. Drain the apples, including the pulp drain. After draining the apples, save the juice. Add 1 cup of sugar to each cup of apple juice into a clean pot. Cook over low heat, stirring often for about an hour and a half. Test by putting a little juice in a saucer and see if it jells. It should jell after it cools. If not, continue cooking in 5-minute increments until the jell test succeeds.

When the jelly is thick enough, remove from the heat. Fill sterilized jars with the jelly. Cover tightly and let sit on the counter for a day. Store in a cool, dry place. Refrigerate after opening. This recipe makes about 4- or 5-pint jars.

Strawberry Jam

2 c. strawberries
4 c. sugar
1 pack of Sure-Jell

Crush the strawberries and measure 2 cups exactly. Let sit a few minutes. Add 4 cups of sugar and mix until sugar is dissolved.

Prepare Sure-Jell from package directions. In a small pan, add 3/4 cup of water with Sure-Jell and boil for 2 minutes. Add immediately to the strawberries and stir. Let sit for 1/2 hour. Put in sterilized jars. Let the jars sit on the counter for a day. Freeze.

Strawberry jam is best kept in the freezer until ready to use. I love this jam on chocolate pie.

Pear Preserves

20 medium ripe Bartlett pears
3/4 c. sugar for each cup of pears
1 lemon

Peel and cut the pears into thin slices and larger pieces. Put pears in the pot you will be making preserves in. Stir in sugar and leave to sit overnight. Cook pears on medium simmer for an hour. Add a sliced lemon. Be sure to take seeds out of the lemon before adding to pot. Stir and cook on a low simmer an additional hour, stirring at least every 15 minutes. Skim off the foam that accumulates on top. After stirring the pears, test the liquid by putting a few drops on a saucer. Let it cool a minute. Test to see if it is thick and sticky. Cook for an additional 10 minutes at a time. When liquid has become a little sticky, remove the pot from the heat.

The old folks used to say,
"Hold on to your fork, baby. The best is yet to come."

LIFE IS A DESSERT

5-Flavor Pound Cake

This cake is called 5-flavor pound cake, but I use six if I have them all. I also always use 6 eggs in a pound cake.

2 sticks of butter
1/2 c. Crisco
2 3/4 c. sugar
6 eggs
1 1/2 c. cake flour
1 1/2 c. regular flour
2 tsp. baking powder
1/2 tsp. salt
1 c. milk
1 tsp. each of coconut, vanilla, butter, rum, lemon, and almond

Glaze

1 c. sugar
1/2 c. water
1 each coconut, vanilla, butter, rum, lemon and almond

Tip before starting on cake, I mix the flavors. In 1 cup of milk, I put 1 teaspoon of each flavor and, at the same time, put 1 teaspoon of each flavor in a small pan for the glaze ingredients—sugar, water, and flavorings that will be heated into a syrup.

Sift flours with baking powder and salt at least 3 times and set aside. Cream butter and Crisco together with sugar until creamy. Separate the eggs. Beat egg whites with 2 tablespoons of sugar until stiff and set aside. Add egg yolks to sugar mixture one at a time and beat until well mixed. After all yolks have been added, alternate adding the flour and the milk mixture, ending with flour. Add beaten egg whites and lightly mix.

Use cake cooking spray or grease and flour a pound cake Bundt pan or a 15-inch loaf pan until coated. Add batter and tap pan lightly to remove air bubbles. Bake in 325 degrees F for 1 hour. Test with a toothpick. Cook an additional 15 minutes if toothpick does not come out clean. Do not leave your oven door open too long or peek at the cake too often.

7 Up Pound Cake

1 1/2 c. butter
3 c. sugar
6 large eggs
1 1/2 c. sifted all-purpose flour
1 1/2 c. cake flour
1 tsp. baking powder
1/2 tsp. salt
1 c. 7 Up
1 1/2 tsp. lemon flavor
1 1/2 tsp. vanilla
1 tsp. orange
1 tsp. coconut

Sift flours with baking powder and salt at least 3 times and set aside. Cream butter together with sugar until creamy. Separate the eggs. Beat egg whites with 2 tablespoons of sugar until stiff and set aside. Add egg yolks to sugar mixture one at a time and beat until well mixed. After all yolks have been added, alternate adding the flour and 7 Up to the mixture until all has been added, ending with flour. Add beaten egg whites and lightly mix. Use baking spray or grease and flour a Bundt pan or a 15-inch loaf pan until coated. Add batter and tap pan lightly to remove air bubbles. Bake at 325 degrees F for 1 hour and 15 minutes. Test with toothpick. Cook an additional 10 minutes if toothpick does not come out clean.

Apple Pie with Graham and Pecan Topping

9-inch piecrust
4 sheets of graham crackers
4 large Granny Smith apples
1 c. sugar
1/2 c. brown sugar
1 tbsp. flour
1 tsp. cinnamon
1 tsp. nutmeg
1/2 stick of butter

Peel and slice apples thinly to make 2 full cups. Mix apples with sugar, 2 tablespoons of brown sugar, flour, cinnamon, and nutmeg. Bake the piecrust at 400 degrees F for 4 or 5 minutes until set. Reduce oven temperature to 350 degrees F. Remove from oven and fill with apples.

Mix the remainder of the brown sugar with crushed graham crackers, 1 tablespoon of butter, and 1/2 cup of pecan pieces that have been slightly toasted together. Set aside.

Bake the apple pie for 30 minutes. Remove from oven and sprinkle with crushed graham cracker as topping. Return to the oven and bake for 20 more minutes.

Aunt Hattie's Coconut Custard Pie

3 egg yolks
3/4 c. sugar
1/4 c. flour
1 tbsp. cornstarch
1 tsp. lemon flavor
1 tsp. coconut flavor
1 tsp. vanilla flavor
1 tbsp. butter
1/2 c. coconut
2 c. milk
9-inch piecrust

Mix sugar with salt, cornstarch, and flour. Beat egg yolks until light and frothy. Add 1 tablespoon of the milk into the eggs. Add eggs to sugar mixture and combine until smooth. Add remainder of milk into flour-and-egg mixture and beat until smooth. Cook over low heat for about 15 minutes until thickened. Add flavors. If necessary, beat with hand mixer while cooking. Once custard is thick, add coconut and blend. Pour into a baked piecrust. Return to oven and cook for 15 minutes. Cool until set.

Homemade Piecrust

2 c. flour
1 tsp. salt
1/2 c. Crisco

Use ice water for moisture. Use the Crisco piecrust recipe. It makes a tender crust for this pie. Follow directions for crust.

Mix flour with salt and add in Crisco until it the flour is course. Add water starting a tablespoon at a time, mixing until it comes together. Roll out on wax paper and cook until golden. Add thickened pie filling and return to oven for 15 minutes at 350 degrees F. Cool completely before cutting.

Aunt Velma's Coconut Cake

This was Uncle Cliff's favorite cake. He would pinch a piece at every opportunity. He was so funny. My aunt always baked the best cakes, tender and light and always exactly right. My uncle Cliff was a character, and he loved her cakes. He would walk through the kitchen and try to sneak a slice of cake and go out the back door. When Uncle Cliff woke up after his surgery at the Veterans Hospital, he decided to call 911 from Veterans Affairs to have the ambulance come to get him out of there. Somebody, please give this man some cake.

2 1/2 c. cake flour, sifted	1 1/4 tsp. lemon
2 1/2 c. baking powder	1 tsp. coconut
1 3/4 c. sugar	2 tbsp. butter
5 eggs	1 c. Crisco
1 tsp. vanilla	1 c. milk

Mix butter and Crisco until creamy. Add sugar 1 cup at a time, mixing thoroughly after each addition. Add egg yolks one at a time and mix thoroughly after each. Add flavors to the cup of milk. Sift cake flour with baking powder and salt at least three times. Beat egg whites until stiff, adding 2 tablespoons of sugar as you beat and set aside. Alternate adding flour and milk to the butter-sugar mixture, making sure to mix in completely after each addition. After all flour and milk has been added, fold in beaten egg whites until just blended. Put into 3 9-inch cake pans that have been greased and floured or sprayed with baking spray. Bake cake for 18 to 22 minutes at 350 degrees F. Frost with the buttercream recipe on Page 186.

Banana Pudding

*This recipe has a smooth custard, but not too thick. It should
have the consistency of gravy, not oatmeal.*

2 or 3 ripe but firm bananas
Nabisco vanilla wafers
2/3 c sugar
1/3 c. flour
1/2 tsp. salt

2 tsp. vanilla
3 egg yolks
1 egg
2 1/2 c. milk

An 8- or 9-inch pie plate or casserole is a good size for this recipe. If you like, you can use 2 individual casserole dishes. Layer bananas sliced in casserole and cover with wafers. Repeat to have 2 layers. Line wafers along the side if you like.

For the pudding

Separate eggs. Put yolks in a small bowl and discard whites or use for a meringue to top the pudding if you like. You can also refrigerate the whites for another use. Add the whole egg to the yolks and beat until lemony and frothy.

In a medium saucepan, mix flour, sugar, and salt together. Add 2 tablespoons of milk to egg yolks. Beat slightly with a fork for at least a minute. This will help the yolks mix well with the flour. Add the yolks to the flour mixture and stir until smooth. Add the rest of the milk a little at a time, about 1/2 cup each time. When all the milk has been added, cook on a low flame, stirring often for about 8 to 10 minutes until the custard starts to thicken. Watch carefully. The custard will be a little thin at this point, but keep in mind that the longer you cook it, the thicker it will get. When it starts to coat the spoon, it is done enough for me.

I like more of a sauce than a custard for my pudding. The custard thickens as it cools. If you prefer a thick custard, just cook it a few more minutes. Stir in vanilla. Remember that the thicker it is, the more like a pudding it will be.

Best Pound Cake

1 1/2 c. butter
1/4 tsp. baking soda
3 c. cake flour
1/2 tsp. mace
2 1/4 c. sugar
2 tsp. vanilla
1/2 tsp. salt
8 large eggs, separated
3/4 tsp. cream of tartar

Take eggs and the butter out of the refrigerator so they can come to room temperature.

Cream butter until light and creamy. Add sugar. Make a little well in the center then beat in yolks one at time. After all the yolks have been added, stir in vanilla and lemon juice. Sift in flour, mace, baking soda, and salt. Add 1/2 cup at a time, beating well after each addition. Beat for at least 10 minutes.

Beat egg whites with cream of tartar until stiff peaks form. Fold into creamed mixture. Bake at 300 degrees F for 2 hours or until done. Turn off oven but leave it in for 30 minutes. Take out and leave in pan for a few minutes. When cooled, transfer onto wax paper.

Butter Rolls

*My cousin Jim A is the one who reminded me of his mother, Couzin Lucille,
who made these butter rolls for the kids. They always looked forward to it.*

2 c. flour
1 tsp. baking powder
1/2 tsp. salt
1/2 c. Crisco
1/2 c. cold water
1/2 c. unsalted butter, very soft
1/4 c. sugar
1/2 tsp. nutmeg

Preheat the oven to 350 degrees F. Lightly spray or grease and flour a 9 x 13 inch pan or casserole baking dish.

In a large bowl, cut the shortening into the flour using two forks, like making biscuits. Add the water and stir until combined. Knead dough onto a lightly floured and sugared surface and roll the dough out thinly, like making a piecrust. Spread soft butter all over the dough then sprinkle with sugar and nutmeg evenly. Carefully and tightly, roll the dough up, jelly roll style, and pinch to seal the long edge. Cut the dough into even-size rolls with a sharp knife and place them into a buttered dish.

For the sauce

2 c. milk
2/3 c. sugar
1 tsp. vanilla extract
1/2 tsp. lemon

For the sauce, combine the milk and sugar in a pot over medium high heat. Stir until the milk just begins to bubble. Remove from the heat and stir in the vanilla and lemon. Pour the mixture over the rolls. Sprinkle with cinnamon if desired. Bake uncovered for 35–45 minutes or until the rolls are brown on top. Serve warm.

Caramel Cake

This was my grandson Jarret's absolute favorite hands down. He would say, "Grandma, Grandma, how about a caramel cake for dessert Sunday?" Then one day, Jazz, who we told not to cut the cake when we left the room, got a fork, sat down at the table, and started eating the whole cake. Well, she didn't cut it.

Caramel frosting 1

    1 stick plus 1 tbsp. butter
    1 1/2 c. brown sugar
    1/2 tsp. salt
    1 tbsp. vanilla
    1 can Eagle Brand milk
    1/2 small can PET Milk

Melt butter and add salt. Add brown sugar and stir to thoroughly mix. When stirring, tilt the pan a little so the brown sugar goes to one side. Then you can see the bottom of the pan. Add 1 teaspoon of vanilla and stir (adding a little vanilla here will intensify it because it gets hot by itself). Add an entire can of Eagle Brand milk, stirring until all is mixed. Start with 1/4 cup of PET milk and cook on low heat, stirring constantly for about 1/2 hour. Add vanilla and remainder of the PET milk and cook for an additional 15 minutes. It's important to keep the frosting stirred to avoid burning. This frosting requires close watching and stirring. Frosting should be smooth and shiny with no lumps. Cool.

I usually set the pot in the freezer for a few minutes. You can frost a hot cake as soon as the frosting is done, and this frosting will make a thin shell, which I prefer. You may want it thicker. When frosting has cooled to room temperature, add 1 cup of powdered sugar. If you like a frosting the consistency of buttercream, add another cup of powdered sugar. Beat until creamy.

Caramel frosting 2

1 stick butter
1 1/2 c. brown sugar
1/2 tsp. salt
1 c. PET milk
2 c. powdered sugar

Melt butter and stir in salt and brown sugar. Stir until sugar is dissolved into butter. Slowly add milk, half a cup at a time. Cook, stirring often, until silky smooth and shiny for about 15 or 20 minutes. Remove from heat. Cool.

I usually put this in the freezer for a few minutes. Add confectionary sugar 1/2 cup at a time, beating with hand mixer until each addition is thoroughly added. Frost using a thin layer on a warm cake or frost a little thicker for a cooled cake.

Cheating Chocolate Cake with Whipped Cream

1 box Duncan Hines Devil's Food cake mix
1/4 c. mayo
1/4 c. butter
1 c. black coffee
3 large eggs, beaten

Whipping cream for middle layer

1/2 pint whipping cream (chill bowl in freezer)
1/4 c. powdered sugar

Whip together in a cold small bowl until stiff.

Chocolate Frosting

1/2 c. cocoa
2 1/2 c. powdered sugar
1/2 stick of butter
1 tsp. vanilla
2 tbsp. black coffee
pinch of salt

Bake cake per directions on box. Cool. Whip the heavy cream until stiff. On the first layer, spread the stiff whipping cream to the edge of the layer. Make chocolate frosting by adding butter to cocoa first. Cream and then add coffee. Add salt and 1 cup of sugar at a time, beating with mixer consistently until creamy but still a little stiff. Add cream a tablespoon at a time with sugar if too stiff. Add milk or whipping cream as needed to get desired consistency.

Cherry Cobbler

1 large 21 oz. can of cherry pie filling
1/3 c. sugar
1/2 tsp. almond or vanilla extract
a pinch of salt

Crust

1/2 c. flour
1/2 c. milk
1/2 c. sugar
1/4 tsp. salt
1/2 stick of butter
1 tsp. vanilla

Mix 1/3 cup of sugar and almond or vanilla flavoring into 1 can of cherry pie filling. Add a pinch of salt and stir until combined. Add 1/4 cup of water and stir again.

Combine flour, milk, sugar, salt, and vanilla together in bowl. Heat the butter in an 8-inch square pan or casserole dish and bake in the oven at 375 degrees F. (The butter must be melted and sizzling hot.) Remove pan from oven and immediately pour batter mixture into hot butter. Then spoon cherry filling on top quickly. *Do not mix.* Just spoon it in quickly. The baking will make the batter spread. Return pan to oven and lower temperature to 350 degrees F. Cook for 35 to 45 minutes until golden on top.

Chocolate Chip Cookies

1/2 c. white sugar
1 1/4 c. flour
1/2 c. butter
1/2 c. brown sugar
1 tsp. vanilla
1/2 tsp. almond
1 egg
1/4 c. pecans
1/2 to 1 c. chocolate chips

Blend sugars with butter until combined. Add lightly beaten egg and flavors and mix well. Add flour into well incorporated. Add chips and pecans. Place on an ungreased cookie sheet and bake at 375 degrees F for 8–10 minutes until lightly browned. I like a crispy cookie, so I add another minute or two.

Cornmeal Cookies Flying Saucers

It's my favorite Milwaukee public school lunch cookies.

4 c. sifted flour
3/4 c. yellow cornmeal
1 1/2 tsp. salt
2 tbsp. baking powder

2 c. butter
2 3/4 c. sugar
3 eggs
1 tbsp. vanilla extract

Sift and mix flour, corn meal, salt, and baking powder. Cream butter and add sugar gradually. Beat until fluffy. Add eggs one at a time and mix well. Add the extract and mix. Add sifted dry ingredients. Spoon cookie dough onto ungreased baking sheets about 3 inches apart. Bake at 350 degrees F for 15 minutes. This make 3 1/2 dozen cookies.

Chocolate Cream Pie

3/4 c. sugar

1/3 c. flour or 3 tbsp. cornstarch

1/4 tsp. salt

2 c. sweet milk

2 squares of unsweetened chocolate

3 egg yolk

2 tbsp. butter

1 tsp. vanilla

9-inch piecrust baked

Mix sugar, salt, and flour in a saucepan. Beat egg yolk with a little milk using a fork until well beaten. Add to sugar, making a smooth paste. Add the rest of the milk slowly, mixing well between intervals. Add some of the mixture to the egg yolk then add to the pan. Cook over low heat. Add chocolate and cook until thickened. Add vanilla. Pour the mixture to the crust and bake for 15 minutes. If using meringue, see directions below. Cool until set.

Meringue

3 or 4 egg whites

1/2 tsp. cream of tartar

1/2 c. sugar

1/2 tsp. vanilla

Beat egg whites and cream of tartar at high speed with electric mixer just until foamy. Gradually add sugar and beat for 3 or 4 minutes until stiff peaks form. Add vanilla and blend. Cover pie completely and bake until meringue is golden brown.

Chocolate Custard Pie

9-inch pie shell, baked
3 egg yolks, beaten
3/4 c. sugar
1/2 tsp. salt
1/3 c. flour
1 tsp. cornstarch
2 tbsp. cocoa
1 tbsp. vanilla
2 1/4 c. milk
1 tbsp. butter

Bake pie shell at 400 degrees F for about 8 minutes until lightly brown. Watch carefully and turn about halfway through baking time. Reduce oven to 350 degrees F. Set aside.

Mix sugar, flour, salt, cornstarch, and cocoa in a medium saucepan. Beat egg yolks lightly with a fork and add 2 tablespoons of milk. Beat until well combined. Mix yolks with sugar mixture until you make a smooth paste. Add the rest of the milk slowly, stirring to keep smooth. Cook over low heat until mixture is thick and creamy. Add vanilla and butter. Stir until the butter melts. Fill the pie shell and bake for 15 minutes at 350 degrees F. Remove and let cool for at least 2 hours before cutting. Serve with whipped cream.

If you want to try it my way, put a spoon of strawberry jam on top, next to the whipped cream. Or if you prefer, cover with a meringue made from egg whites.

Coconut Cream Tart

1/2 c. flour
3/4 c. sugar
4 large eggs
2 c. milk
1 tbsp. vanilla
1 tsp. coconut flavor
1 c. coconut

Tart shells

2 1/2 c. flour
3/4 c. cold butter
1/2 tsp. salt
2 tbsp. cold water

Stir together 1/3 cup of flour and 3/4 cup of sugar. Beat eggs and combine with flour mixture. Add 1/4 cup of milk until smooth. Add additional milk a little at a time until all milk is added and the mixture is smooth. Cook over low heat. Stir constantly over medium heat until mixture thickens. Add vanilla and 1 cup of coconut. Let cool and then chill completely before adding to the shells.

Prepare tart shell dough and divide among small pans. Prick the bottom. Freeze for about 20 minutes until cold. Bake at 375 degrees F until lightly browned. Cool and then add cream to each shell. Sprinkle coconut on top of each tart.

Cream Cheese Danish Cake

My friend Shirley from Wisconsin bakes these decadent Danish cakes every time she knows I am visiting Milwaukee and sends them home with me for my husband. It used to be for both of us, but it gradually became his. They freeze well and can be microwaved a few seconds to warm them enough to enjoy.

1 pkg. Red Star Quick Rise dry yeast
1/4 c. warm water
2 1/2 c. all-purpose flour
1 tbsp. sugar
1 tsp. salt
4 egg yolks
1 c. butter
2 8 oz. pkg. cream cheese, softened
1 c. sugar
1 egg yolk
1 egg white, slightly beaten
1/2 c. chopped nuts (optional)

Glaze

1 c. powdered sugar
1 tsp. vanilla
2 to 3 tbsp. water

In a small bowl, dissolve yeast in warm water. Let it stand for 5 minutes. In large bowl, combine flour, 1 tablespoon of sugar, and salt. Mix well. With pastry blender, cut in butter until the consistency of cornmeal. Add dissolved yeast and 4 beaten egg yolks to flour mixture. Mix lightly with fork. Shape dough into a ball. Cover bowl with plastic wrap and foil and refrigerate for 2 hours. (This is an extraordinarily rich dough and will rise very little.)

Meanwhile, prepare the filling. Beat cream cheese, 1 cup sugar, and egg yolk until smooth. Set aside.

After dough is risen, divide into 2 parts. On lightly floured surface, roll each half in to a 15 x 10 inch rectangle. Roll rectangle onto rolling pin and transfer to greased jelly roll pan. Spread filling over dough. Roll the rest of the dough into a 15 x 10 inch rectangle and carefully place over top of the filling. Brush top with egg white. Sprinkle with nuts if desired. Let rise in warm place for 1 hour. Bake at 350 degrees F for 25 to 30 minutes.

Prepare glaze by combining ingredients until smooth. Drizzle glaze over warm coffeecake cut into squares or bars. Store in refrigerator.

Crisco Pie Crust

This piecrust is light and good for most custard fillings.

2 c. flour
2/3 c. Crisco
1 tsp. salt
4 tbsp. ice water

Sift flour and salt together. Add Crisco and mix until it is the consistency of a coarse meal. Add ice water, starting with about 3 tablespoons. Blend with a fork until it stays together. Make a disc and chill for at least half an hour. Roll out between 2 pieces of wax paper until it fits in the pie pan. Prebake piecrust until just set.

Double Chocolate Custard Pie

2 9-inch pie shells, baked
6 egg yolks, beaten
1 1/2 c. sugar
1/2 tsp. salt
2/3 c. flour
41/2 tbsp. cocoa
2 tbsp. vanilla
41/2 c. milk
2 tbsp. butter

Bake pie shell at 400 degrees F for 8 minutes until lightly brown. Reduce the heat to 350 degrees F.

Mix sugar, flour, salt, cornstarch, and cocoa in pan. Beat egg yolks until light and add 2 tablespoons of milk. Mix yolks with sugar mixture until you make a smooth paste. Add the rest of the milk slowly, stirring to keep smooth. Cook until mixture is thick and creamy. Add vanilla and butter. Stir until butter melts. Fill pie shells and bake for 15 minutes in 350 degrees F. Remove and let cool for at least 2 hours before cutting. Serve with whipped cream.

Easy Cheesecake Pie

Martha's favorite. These very easy cheesecake pies are not so quick, but worth the effort.

Version 1 (Crystal)

  1 8 oz. pkg. Philadelphia cream cheese, softened
  1 1/2 tsp. Crystal Light Lemonade flavor soft drink mix
  zest of 1 lemon
  1/4 c. cold 2% milk
  1 8 oz. tub Cool Whip sugar free
  1 ready-to-use cookie crust

Beat cream cheese, drink mix, and lemon zest in large bowl. Mix until well blended. Gradually add milk, mixing well. Gently stir in Cool Whip. Spoon into crust and chill until firm or freeze if desired.

Version 2

  1 can Eagle Brand condensed milk
  1 6 oz. frozen lemonade
  1 8 oz. Cool Whip
  1 cookie crust

Mix milk, lemonade, and cool whip thoroughly. Add to crust and freeze for 2 hours.

Fried Apple Pies

3 Granny Smith apples
3/4 c. sugar
1 tbsp. flour
1 tsp. cinnamon
2 tbsp. butter
1 tbsp. vanilla
1/2 tsp. lemon
1/4 tsp. nutmeg

Slice apples thinly and cook in over low heat in a couple spoons of water. The apples should be tender. Add remaining ingredients. Butter will melt when added to hot apples. Stir to combine.

Make up piecrust and roll out or use cut piecrust sheets into small discs. You should get 3 or 4 good-size discs. Roll out thinly but make sure it still holds together. Put apple mixture on 1/2 of disc and fold over. Press the edges tightly. Melt the butter and Crisco on the skillet and fry the pies. Carefully turn when one side is brown. You can also add to the baking sheet. Lightly brush with additional butter and sprinkle sugar on top. Bake at 350 degrees F until golden brown.

Ella's Egg Pie

3 eggs
1 can of PET milk, well shaken
1 1/2 c. sugar
1 tsp. nutmeg
1 tsp. vanilla
1 tsp. lemon
1 tbsp. flour
1 tbsp. cornstarch
pinch of salt

Combine sugar, flour, salt, cornstarch, and nutmeg. Beat eggs thoroughly until light and fluffy. Add PET milk and beat with hand mixer until well blended. Add slowly to flour mixture and beat until smooth. Partially bake piecrust for 5 or 6 minutes at 375 degrees F. Add filling to crust. It is a little easier to work with if you can quickly add the filling to the crust while it is in the oven. Make sure your rack is in far enough to be level, but out far enough to pour without getting burned. Lower oven temperature to 350 degrees F. Bake for at least 45 minutes until slightly golden. Pie may still jiggle a little in the center. It will be firmer as it cools.

German Chocolate Cake (Original)
with Coconut Pecan Filling and Chocolate Frosting

This is my husband's favorite birthday and holiday cake.

2 c. unsifted all-purpose flour or cake flour
1 1/2 c. sugar
1 tsp. baking soda
1/2 tsp. baking powder
1/2 tsp. salt
2/3 c. butter
1 c. buttermilk
1 tsp. vanilla
2 eggs
1 package German's sweet chocolate (melted)

Mix flour with sugar, soda, baking powder, and salt. Stir butter to soften. Add flour mixture, buttermilk, vanilla, eggs, and chocolate. Beat for 3 minutes at medium speed with a mixer, making sure to scrape the bowl often to get everything mixed smooth.

Spray with baking spray or grease and flour two 9-inch cake pans. Fill pans. Tap pans lightly against the counter. Preheat oven to 350 degrees F and bake for 25 minutes. Turn onto wax paper and cool. Spread the bottom and top with pecan frosting and frost the sides with chocolate frosting.

Coconut pecan filling

1 stick of butter
1 c. sugar
1/2 tsp. salt
3 egg yolks
1 c. PET milk
1 tsp. vanilla
1 c. pecans
1 c. coconut

Mix and cook until thick. Stir often for about 12 to 15 minutes. Chill (put in freezer until cold).

Chocolate Frosting

1/2 c. cocoa
2 1/2 c. powdered sugar
1/2 stick of butter
1 tsp. vanilla
2 tbsp. black coffee
1 tbsp. milk
pinch of salt

Quick Version of Cake

Duncan Hines German Chocolate Cake mix

1/2 c. butter
1 c. black coffee (or 1/2 coffee 1/2 milk)
3 large eggs, beaten

Bake cake per directions on box, substituting milk or coffee for water and butter for oil. Cool. Make pecan filling and cool. On the first layer, spread the pecan filling to the edge of the layer without overlapping. Make chocolate frosting by adding butter to cocoa first. Cream and then add coffee. Add salt and 1 cup of sugar at a time, beating with mixer consistently until creamy but still a little stiff. Add cream a tablespoon at a time alternately with sugar. Add milk or whipping cream as needed to get desired consistency. Spread on cool side of the cake, being careful not to mix with pecan filling

Holiday Beauty Layer Cake
with Buttercream Frosting

green and red food coloring
2 1/2 c. sifted cake flour
2 tsp. baking powder
1/2 tsp. salt
1 stick of butter (room temperature)
1/2 c. Crisco
2 c. sugar
4 large egg yolks
4 large egg whites
2 tsp. vanilla
1 tsp. almond
1 c. milk

Sift together the flour, baking powder, and salt. Set aside. Beat egg whites with 2 tablespoons of sugar until stiff and set aside. Cream butter and beat until fluffy and light. Add sugar and beat until well mixed and creamy. Add egg yolks 1 at a time, beating after each addition. Add vanilla and almond into the milk. Alternate adding flour and milk into the mixture until all is incorporated. Fold in egg whites. Divide batter into two parts. Add green food coloring to one bowl and red food coloring to the other. Spray two 9-inch cake pans with baking spray or grease with Crisco and flour. Divide cake batter in pans. Bake at 350 degrees F for 18–23 minutes. Test with toothpick. If the toothpick comes out clean, it is done. Place onto wax paper to cool.

Buttercream Frosting

1 stick of butter
1/2 tsp. salt
1 tsp. vanilla
1/2 tsp. coconut
4 c. powdered sugar
4 tbsp. PET milk (add more if needed)

Cream butter and blend with all other ingredients until smooth. Frost cake with frosting and sprinkle with coconut on the side and top layer.

Homemade Layer Cake

1 stick plus 1 tbsp. of butter
1/2 c. Crisco
2 c. sugar
4 eggs, separated
1 c. milk
2 1/2 c. cake flour
2 tsp. baking powder
1/2 tsp. salt
1 tbsp. vanilla
1 tsp. lemon
1/2 tsp. almond

Separate eggs, putting egg whites into small mixing bowl and yolks in another bowl. Beat egg whites with 2 tablespoons of sugar until stiff and set aside.

Sift cake flour with baking powder and salt at least three times. Set aside.

Mix butter and Crisco until creamy. Add sugar 1 cup at a time, mixing thoroughly after each addition. Add egg yolks one at a time and mix well. Add flavors to the cup of milk. Alternate adding flour and milk to the butter-sugar mixture, making sure to mix in thoroughly after each addition. After all flour and milk has been added, fold in beaten egg whites until just blended.

Do not beat batter.

Put into three 9-inch cake pans that have been greased and floured or sprayed with baking spray. Bake for 18 to 22 minutes at 350 degrees F.

Key Lime Icebox Pie

2 8 oz. pkg. of cream cheese
1 can Eagle Brand milk
1 tub sugar-free Cool Whip
1/2 c. fresh lime juice
2 tbsp. lime concentrate
1 tbsp. lime zest
2 tbsp. green crème de menthe (if not available, use juice)
1/4 tsp. salt
1 Keebler cookie crust

Zest 6 limes and then juice them. If not quite a 1/2 cup of juice add bottled lime juice to make 1/2 cup of juice. Beat cream cheese until smooth. Add milk and combine well. Add lime zest, crème de menthe, and juices to cream cheese. Mix well. Fold in Cool Whip that is slightly thawed, *not* room temperature. Fill crust and freeze for at least 3 hours. Garnish with lime slice sprinkled with sugar. Serve frozen or slightly thawed.

Mississippi Chess Pie

1 stick of butter, softened
4 eggs
1 1/2 c. sugar
1/2 tsp. salt
1 tbsp. corn meal
1 tbsp. white vinegar
1 tsp. vanilla
1 tsp. lemon
9-inch pie shell

Partially bake pie shell at 375 degrees F for about 4 to 6 minutes or until very lightly browned. Watch carefully. Reduce oven to 325 degrees F. Mix butter, sugar, and meal with hand mixer. Beat the eggs with salt until it is light and fluffy. Add eggs to sugar mixture, beating slowly. Add vinegar and flavors. Pour into pie shell and continue to bake for 45 minutes.

Mama's Coconut Pineapple Cake

This cake is very moist and keeps well. Because of the pineapple filling, it should be kept in the refrigerator.

Cake

2 1/4 c. sifted cake flour
2 tsp. baking powder
1/2 tsp. salt
2 sticks of butter (room temperature)
2 c. sugar
2 tsp. vanilla
1 tsp. coconut
1 c. coconut milk or regular milk
4 large egg yolks
4 large egg whites

Sift together the flour, baking powder, and salt. Set aside. Beat egg whites with 2 tablespoons of sugar until stiff and set aside. Cream butter and beat until fluffy and light. Add sugar and beat until well mixed and creamy. Add egg yolks 1 at a time, beating after each addition. Add vanilla. Alternate adding flour and milk into the mixture until all is incorporated. Fold in egg whites. Spray two 9-inch cake pans with baking spray or grease with Crisco and flour. Divide cake batter in pans. Bake at 350 degrees F for 18–23 minutes. Test with toothpick. If the toothpick comes out clean, it is done.

Glaze

3 c. powdered sugar
1/3 c. butter
1 tsp. vanilla
3 tbsp. PET milk (adding additional to get desired consistency)
1 tbsp. coconut milk (if you have it)
a pinch of salt

Pineapple Sauce

Mix 1 small can of crushed pineapple drained into small saucepan with 1 teaspoon of flour and 2 teaspoon of cornstarch. Add 1 cup of sugar. Cook over medium flame, stirring constantly for 15 minutes or until mixture is thick and smooth. Cool. Add as filling on top of a thin layer of frosting in the middle layers. This is a very moist cake.

Mama's Old-Fashioned Tea Cakes

Tea cakes are always hard after the first day, but we loved them anyway. Usually, there were not many left over.

2 sticks of butter
2 tbsp. Crisco
2 c. sugar
2 c. cake flour
2 c. flour
2 1/2 tsp. baking powder
1/2 tsp. salt
1/4 c. milk
4 egg yolks plus 1 whole egg
1 tbsp. vanilla
1 tbsp. lemon
1 1/2 tsp. nutmeg
1/2 tsp. cinnamon

Cream butter with sugar. Beat egg yolks and whole egg together until frothy. Beat into sugar mixture until creamy. Add milk. Beat in flavor and nutmeg for about 2 minutes until well blended.

Sift flour with salt, baking powder, and pinch of cinnamon. Add to cream mixture until stiff enough to roll out for cutting. On wax or parchment paper, sprinkle enough flour to roll out the dough without sticking. As you work in the flour, you may have to continue to add a little at a time until you can roll them out without sticking. Cut with biscuit cutter or a small glass and place on an ungreased cookie sheet. Bake at 350 degrees F until lightly browned.

Tea cakes will harden as they cool. To keep them softer, store with a few slices of white bread in between them. If you heat them in the microwave for a few seconds, they will be just like fresh baked.

Whipping Cream Pound Cake

I love an original whipping cream pound cake with caramel frosting, but the homemade recipe below is also great.

3 sticks of butter
3 c. sugar
6 eggs
1 tbsp. vanilla
1 tsp. almond
3 c. cake flour, sifted
1/2 tsp. baking powder
1/2 tsp. salt
1 c. whipping cream

Cream butter and sugar until well blended. Add eggs one at a time. (I always use a hand mixer so I can beat the egg in the bowl lightly before incorporating it into the sugar mixture. Just make a well on the side or middle.) Then beat very well after each addition. Alternate adding flour and milk to the butter-sugar mixture, making sure to mix in completely after each addition. After all flour and milk has been added, fold in beaten egg whites until just blended. Bake at 325 degrees F in a Bundt cake pan or use a 16 x 4 inch rectangle pound cake pan for about 55 minutes. Check for doneness with a toothpick.

Martha's favorite

Oatmeal Crispies Cookies

1 stick of butter
1/2 c. brown sugar
1/2 c. white sugar
1 egg, lightly beaten
1 tbsp. molasses
1/2 tsp. almond

1 tsp. vanilla
1 1/2 c. oatmeal
3/4 c. flour
1/2 tsp. salt
1/2 tsp. baking soda
1/2 c. toasted pecans or walnuts

Mix sugars with butter. Add egg and mix well. Add molasses and flavor to the mixture. Sift in the flour with baking soda and salt. Mix in nuts with oatmeal before adding to the flour mixture. Add flour and oats to butter mixture and pour onto ungreased cookie sheet in equal parts. Bake at 375 degrees F for 11 minutes.

Old-Fashioned Pound Cake

4 c. powdered sugar (1 lb. box)
2 c. butter
2 tbsp. freshly grated orange zest
6 eggs
2 c. flour
1 1/2 c. cake flour
2 tsp. vanilla
1/2 tsp. baking powder
1/2 tsp. salt

Sift the sugar. Cream the butter on medium speed with hand mixer for about 3 minutes or until light and fluffy. Gradually add sugar, about half a cup at a time and the orange zest. Beat thoroughly. Add eggs one at a time, mixing well after adding each egg. Beat the egg in the bowl a little well before incorporating into the batter.

Sift the flours with salt and baking powder 3 times. Add the flour mixture into the batter 1 cup at a time, mixing well after each addition. Pour into a greased and floured Bundt pan. Bake at 350 degrees F for 1 hour and 20 minutes. Remove from the pan and cool.

Old Virginia Pound Cake

2 sticks of butter
1/2 c. Crisco
3 c. sugar
5 eggs
3 c. cake flour
1 c. milk
1 tsp. vanilla
1 tsp. lemon
dash of nutmeg (if desired)

No baking powder or soda is used in this recipe. Sift the sugar. Cream butter and Crisco on medium speed with a hand mixer for about 3 minutes until light and fluffy. Gradually add sugar and flavorings. Cream thoroughly. Add eggs one at a time, mixing well after adding each egg. (Beat the egg in the bowl in a little before incorporating into the batter.)

Sift the flour 3 times. Add flour 1 cup at a time, alternating with some of the milk. Mix well after each addition. Pour into greased and floured Bundt pan. Bake at 350 degrees F for 1 hour and 20 minutes. Remove from the pan to cool.

Orange Cream Cheese Pound Cake

1 1/2 c. butter (3 sticks)
1 8 oz. cream cheese
3 c. sugar
6 large eggs
1/2 tsp. baking soda
1/2 tsp. baking powder
1 1/2 c. sifted all-purpose flour
1 1/2 c. cake flour
1/2 tsp. salt
1 tbsp. orange zest
1 tsp. vanilla
juice from 1 orange (no more than 1/4 c.)

Cream butter until it is fluffy and light. Add sugar and cream until well mixed and volume is increased. Add eggs one at a time, mixing into sugar mixture completely before adding each egg. (I make a little indention by taking the back of the spoon then add each egg and beat it before beating it into the butter-and-sugar mixture.) After adding all the eggs, sift flours, salt, and baking powder. Add some flavor and the juice. Bake at 325 degrees F for 1 hour and 15 min.

If desired, make a glaze with 1 cup of powdered sugar, 1/2 teaspoon of orange zest, and 2 tablespoons of milk. Spread over the cake.

Original Pound Cake

1 lb. butter
1 lb. confectioner's sugar
12 eggs, separated
4 1/2 c. flour
1/2 tsp. salt
1/2 tsp. nutmeg
1 tsp. vanilla
2 tbsp. grated lemon zest
1/2 c. whipping cream

Separate the eggs. Add whites to a small mixing bowl that is large enough to whip the whites in.

Sift flour, nutmeg, and 1/2 teaspoon of salt. Set aside.

Beat egg whites until stiff with 2 tablespoons of sugar and set aside.

Cream butter with sugar. Then add egg yolks to butter and sugar. Beat with a mixer until creamy and smooth. Add the lemon zest and 1 teaspoon of vanilla. Add flour mixture 1/2 cup at a time, alternating with a little cream until all flour and cream has been mixed in. The mixture will be thick. When all flour has been added, fold in whipped egg whites until the streaks have almost disappeared. Do not overbeat after adding whites. Bake at 325 degrees F for 1 hour.

Peach and Pear Cobbler (2 Ways)

2 small cans of peaches
1 can of sliced pears
1 tbsp. flour
1 tbsp. cornstarch
1 1/2 c. sugar
1/2 tsp. salt
1 tbsp. cinnamon
1/2 stick of butter

Cut up peaches and pears in bite-size pieces. Put the fruits with their juice plus 1/2 cup of water into a medium saucepan. Blend flour, cornstarch, and salt with 2 tablespoons of water until smooth. Add the mixture to the fruits and stir to combine. Add sugar and cinnamon to the pot and boil. Add butter and let it simmer for about 5 minutes. Pour into a casserole dish.

Crust 1

1 1/2 c. Bisquick
1 tsp. baking powder
1/2 cinnamon
1/2 c. melted butter
1/4 c. milk

Combine all ingredients, except milk, until the mix is almost all crumbly. Add milk a tablespoon at a time until dough holds together and can be rolled out between 2 sheets of waxed paper. Roll as thin as you can because it will rise some while baking. Fill casserole with fruit mixture. Cut dough into strips and lay on top of the fruit. Cut small pieces of butter and dot all over the top. Sprinkle with additional sugar and bake at 350 degrees F until top is brown and fruit is bubbly.

Crust 2

Prepare the fruits the same as above, omitting the butter.

Mix 1 cup flour, 1 cup sugar, and 1 cup milk together with 1 teaspoon salt and 1 teaspoon baking powder until smooth. In a 9 x 13 casserole dish or pan, heat 1 stick of butter until it sizzles. Let the butter brown a little. The butter *must* be extremely hot. Pour batter mix in casserole immediately and pour fruit mixture on top. Bake in 350 degrees F for 45 minutes. The batter will rise to the top and form a crust if the butter is hot.

Peanut Butter Cookies

1/2 c. butter or Crisco
1/2 c. sugar
1/2 c. brown sugar
1/2 c. peanut butter
1 egg, lightly beaten
1 tsp. vanilla
1 1/4 c. flour
1/2 tsp. baking soda
1/2 tsp. salt
1/2 c. peanuts, chopped

Mix butter or butter flavored Crisco with sugars and combine until smooth. Add beaten egg and blend. Add peanut butter, peanuts, and vanilla. Sift in flour, baking soda, and salt together. Add to the butter mixture until flour is totally incorporated. Bake on ungreased cookie sheet by the tablespoonful and press down slightly with a fork. Sprinkle with sea salt. Bake at 375 degrees F for 12–15 minutes.

Pecan Tarts

Tart shell

    3 sticks of butter
    1 c. sugar
    1 tsp. vanilla
    1/2 tsp. salt
    3 1/2 c. flour

Mix together all ingredients and chill. Pinch enough to fill each mini muffin tin until full. Make filling and fill tin.

Pecan filling

    1 egg plus 1 yolk
    1/2 c. brown sugar
    1/2 c. syrup
    1 tbsp. molasses
    1/2 c. butter
    1 c. broken pecans
    1 tsp. vanilla
    1/4 tsp. salt

Melt butter in saucepan and stir in sugar, syrup, and molasses. Beat egg and yolk with 1/4 teaspoon salt. Spoon a couple of sugar mixture into the eggs. Beat well. Add back into butter mix. Add pecans and spoon into tart shells. Add a whole pecan on top. Bake at 350 degrees F for 20 minutes until set in center.

Rice Pudding

Long-grain rice is better for baking in a custard than jasmine.

1 c. long-grain white rice
1 c. water
1 c. milk
1 large or 2 small eggs
1/2 tsp. salt
11/2 c. sugar
1/2 c. raisins or 2 small boxes
1 can PET milk
2 tsp. lemon flavor
1 tbsp. vanilla
1/2 tsp. nutmeg
1 tsp. cinnamon
1/2 c. butter
1/4 to 1/2 c. rum or brandy

Soak raisins in rum or brandy for 15 minutes. In a medium saucepan, combine water and milk with salt and rice. Boil on low heat per package directions for 20 to 25 minutes. Remove from heat. Grease a casserole dish generously with butter. Pour rice into casserole dish and stir in butter and sugar until well combined. Add in raisins with liquor, flavor, and seasoning. Beat the eggs until frothy. Add PET milk to eggs and stir well. Add milk mixture to rice mixture. Add more milk if necessary. Dot with additional pats of butter and sprinkle surface with a small mixture of sugar and cinnamon. Bake at 350 degrees F for 25 minutes. Center should be slightly soft. Eat hot or at room temperature

Southern Sweet Potato Pie

9-inch piecrust
3 eggs
1 can sweet potatoes or 2 medium fresh sweet potatoes
1/2 c. light brown sugar
1/2 c. white sugar
1 tsp. cinnamon
1/2 tsp. ginger
1/2 tsp. nutmeg
1/4 tsp. ground cloves
1/2 tsp. salt
1/4 c. milk
1/2 c. heavy whipping cream

Prebake piecrust until just set. Mash sweet potatoes until creamy. Beat eggs until frothy. Add milk to eggs and beat again. Blend egg mixture into potatoes. Mix all pie seasonings into the mixture with a hand mixer until smooth. Pour into the piecrust. Bake for 60–70 minutes at 350 degrees F.

Sweet Potato Casserole

2 large sweet potatoes
1 stick of butter
1/2 c sugar
1/4 c brown sugar
cinnamon
nutmeg

Slice the sweet potatoes as thinly as you can cut them. Mix white and brown sugar together. Layer the sweet potatoes with pats of butter, sugar, and cinnamon. The layers should be thin, but each one will have butter, sugar, and cinnamon in them. When all the sweet potatoes have been layered, sprinkle with a little brown sugar and nutmeg. Add 2 or 3 tablespoons of water into casserole. Cover tightly and cook in the oven at 350 degrees F for 30 to 45 minutes until fork tender.

Sweet Potato Pie

My brother David loved sweet potato pie. He would always hide it from us and eat it all up. I, with young stupid wisdom, forced him to eat a whole pie at once after he already had one. He got sick and did not eat sweet potato pie for years. We both talk about it, but it was not a good thing to do. Yes, he eats pie again, but only a slice at a time.

2 large sweet potatoes baked until tender

1 c. sugar

1 tbsp. brown sugar

2 eggs, well beaten

1/2 c. butter, softened

1 tsp. nutmeg

1/2 tsp. cinnamon

1/4 tsp. allspice

1 tbsp. vanilla

1 tsp. lemon

2 tbsp. flour

1/2 tsp. salt

1/2 can PET milk

Peel potatoes when cool enough to handle. Mash and take out any strings. Mix with sugars and flour until blended. Add butter and flavors. Mix and taste. Adjust seasoning if necessary. Beat eggs and add milk. Beat until egg and milk are well blended (I use my hand mixer). Add milk with sugar mixture until smooth.

Prebake pie shell until slightly browned. Fill and bake at 400 degrees F for 10 minutes. Reduce oven temperature to 350 degrees F and continue to bake for 30 minutes. It is okay if it is not solid in the middle. It will finish as it cools. Having a homemade pie shell is better. I use the Crisco piecrust recipe.

Tess's Brown Sugar Cookies

I fell in love with these cookies when a wonderful woman I worked with in Milwaukee brought me cookies at least once a week. When she did not bring cookies, she bought me an apple or orange. It was amazing to me that she knew, somehow always knew, that I really appreciated and needed her kindness. Her name was Tess. I would love to give her a hug.

1 c. butter
1 c. brown sugar
1 c. white sugar
2 eggs, lightly beaten
2 tsp. baking soda
1/2 tsp. salt
2 tsp. cream of tartar
1/2 tsp. almond
1 tsp. vanilla (I use 2 tsp.)
3 c. sifted flour

Sift and mix in flour, cream of tartar, baking soda, and salt. Cream butter and sugars until fluffy. Add beaten eggs and flavors. Add flour mixture. Roll the dough into a ball, each about the size of a tablespoon. Roll the balls into a small plate of sugar. Place on ungreased cookie sheet and bake at 400 degrees F for 8–11 minutes

Note, if you have no cream of tartar, you can mix 1/2 teaspoon of baking soda with 1/2 teaspoon of baking powder.

The Family Chess Pie

Cream cheese piecrust

    3 oz. cream cheese
    1 c. flour
    1/2 c. margarine or butter

Mix cream cheese and butter together. Add flour and roll into disk. Chill for 15 minutes. Cook the crust for about 5 minutes at 350 degrees F until just set.

Filling

    3 eggs
    1 3/4 c. sugar
    1 tbsp. meal
    2 tbsp. flour
    1 tbsp. vinegar
    1 stick of butter
    1/2 c. PET milk
    1 tsp. vanilla

Mix butter and sugar. Cream well. Add flour and meal. Add eggs one at a time, beating well after each addition with a hand mixer. Add milk and vanilla. Pour into the piecrust and bake at 350 degrees F. for 50 minutes.

Uncle Heard's Ice Cream

1 can Eagle Brand milk
1/2 gal. milk
2 tbsp. flour
1 1/2 c. sugar
1 tsp. salt
6 egg yolks
2 tbsp. vanilla
2 tbsp. lemon
1 large can PET milk

Mix all milks in a pot. Add flour into 1/4 cup of milk and beat until smooth. Add flour mixture back into milk and stir until well blended. Start heating on low flame. Add sugar and salt to the milk and stir until hot. Beat egg yolks until lemony and smooth. Add a couple of spoons of milk to eggs to temper them while stirring. Add back into milk mixture. Continue to cook, stirring constantly for another 15 minutes. It should thicken slightly as it cooks to the consistency of heavy cream. Add flavor. Take off heat and let it cool.

Refrigerate for at least two hours. To freeze in ice cream maker, pour cream mixture into freezer container and add the dasher. Put container into freezer before alternating chipped or small cube ice and rock salt. Churn until semi frozen. When freezer becomes hard to turn, it's ready. Leave in the freezer until it hardens.

COOLERS

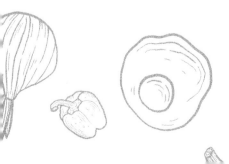

Grasshopper Thick

This is strictly a Martha thing. I love the minty flavor. When making my own, I usually buy some sugar-free ice cream by the half gallon, mix it up, and refreeze. Whenever I want a cold drink, I scoop some out into a beautiful, stemmed glass given to me by my friend Gayle from Jersey. The glass and the drink feels like a well-deserved treat, and I enjoy every drop.

1/2 c. crème de menthe

1/2 c. crème de cocoa

1/2 gal. vanilla ice cream (sugar free is good)

Mix all ingredients in a pitcher or bowl. When this has mixed well, the volume will be less. Pour into serving glasses or add back into the ice cream container and freeze until ready to use. It will pour when first made, but it can also be frozen.

7 Up Sherbet Float

Martha's favorite. When we had the barbeque place, it would get so hot in the summer that I would get some sherbet and 7 Up and make these for us. Simple and good.

2 scoops of any flavor sherbet

1 7 oz. can of 7 Up or Sprite

Spoon sherbet into tall glass and slowly add soda. Serve with a spoon and straw. This makes a great summer dessert or beverage.

COMPANY SPREADS

Cold Cut Plate. Buy deli slices that are not too thin or thick. Roll chicken, ham, roast beef, and salami tightly and place spirally on an oblong or square plate with salami in the center.

Salad Plate. For veggies, add celery, cherry tomatoes, radishes, carrot sticks, broccoli, and julienned cucumber sticks. Try displaying fruit in the middle of your salad tray instead of the outer edges. An elegant Southern buffet for me, even with finger foods, should include olives and bread and butter pickle sticks. Hog's head cheese slices alternated with rows of cold cut slices is an unexpected touch.

Company Coming. When you have unexpected company, there is no need to stress. I light the grill and put on a chicken if I have time. I usually keep a Sam's Club brown sugar ham in the freezer for such times. It is easy to just put in the oven still frozen and glaze when it thaws. If you don't have time just run to the grocery store's deli and bakery and pick up what you need.

- pound cake or cookies
- roast chicken
- sliced baked ham
- potato salad
- fruit plate (includes grapes, whole strawberries, cantaloupe, pineapple, watermelon, and honeydew)

PREPARING WELCOMING BITES

Cut Barbeque Ribs into Individual Bones. Stack into tents after cutting and dip just the top of the rib into the sauce. Lean the bottoms together to make a tent in the middle of your appetizer tray or layer in rows neatly. This way, guests can use tongs to grab. Have several different sauces and hot sauce available.

Thin Roast or Ham-Wrapped Asparagus. Blanch asparagus until crisp tender. Add cold water to stop cooking. Wrap with thinly sliced ham or roast beef from the deli. Before wrapping. I sometimes add a thin line of spicy mustard for extra taste.

Mini Ham and Biscuits with Pepper Jelly. Bake a pan of biscuits, spread with hot pepper jelly, and add a thin slice of ham folded into quarters.

Tuna Croissants. Make tuna salad and chill. Split mini croissants down the side, add a leaf of fresh Bibb lettuce, and stuff with tuna. Do not use lettuce that has wilted.

Cocktail Shrimp. If using shrimp that has been cooked, cleaned, and deveined, leave on a small section of the tail. Rinse in a bowl of cold water with a squeeze of fresh lemon. Fill a bowl with ice and lemon slices. Place a small bowl of cocktail sauce in the center and hang the shrimp around the edges.

CELEBRATION DINNERS

These are dinners, dishes, or desserts that you make especially for you for whatever reason. You really do not have to have a major event. Make every breath worth celebrating. It's kind of like when you finally discover that you are not the problem in a relationship, but you are the only glue holding it together. Or when you look in the mirror and really see just how beautiful, smart, and well put together you have always been. You are not too XYZ or whatever it is you stress over. All your worry is a waste of time. There is no blues the color of your blues, and there is also no blues the color of anybody else's. So celebrate yourself and make yourself a meal of favorites and smile.

My cousin Sally loves to celebrate with a German chocolate cake. Another cousin, Al, loves steak, a baked potato, and strawberry cheesecake. My longtime friend Shirley loves homemade dressing, mac and cheese, and fried chicken if staying close to home. But if she is going out, it's the biggest, best rib eye she can find and a big baked potato.

My favorites are all Cs:

- *collards,*
- *chicken,*
- *caramel cake,*
- *corn bread, and*
- *corn.*

PRAISE SONGS

Ain't nothing like cooking and praising God. When you put on your favorite inspirational music and get started cooking, before you know it, you have cooked up some good dishes.

'Cause, honey, prayer is like sweets for the soul!

I had to include my gospel lists at the end of the book, but I know everyone has their own inspiration specials.

- "Safe in His Arms" by Mervin Mayo
- Dr. Watts hymns by Marvin Williams
- "You Can't Beat God Giving" by Billy Preston
- "Pray for Me" by The Angelic Singers
- "If It Had Not Been for the Lord" By Helen Baylor
- "There's a Leak in the Old Building" By Neal Robinson
- "Never Grow Old" by Aretha Franklin
- "Believe" by Brooks and Dunn
- "Where Is Your Faith in God" by James Cleveland
- "When Will I" by Candi Staton
- "Hymns that brought me through" by LaShun Pace
- "Blessing on Me"
- "Dr. Watts Old Baptist devotional hymns" by Marvin Williams
- "Just for Me" by Inez Andrews
- "Mountains" by Lonestar
- "I'm Still Holding On" by Luther Barnes
- "God's Grace" by Luther Barnes
- "Jesus" by Shirley Caesar
- "Touch Me Lord Jesus" by The Angelic Singers

Praise God!

Here are some pictures of the taste testers, and those responsible for some of these delicious recipes!

Mama Picnicking

Aunt Velma and Jarret

Sally

Martha and Shirley

Husband John, Chief tester and Martha

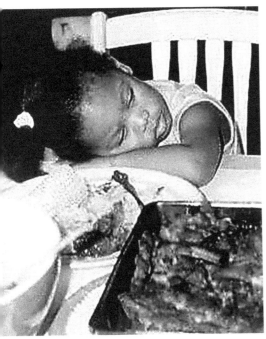 

Jazz and Donnis

Hattie, Thelma, Aunt Velma, and Cordie

Donnis, Mama, and Martha

Cordie, Martha, and Barbara

INDEX

Collard Greens
Fried Corn
Fried Green Tomatoes
Fried Okra
Fried Sweet Potatoes
Green Beans and Potatoes
Grilled Corn
Onion Rings
Pan-Fried Squash
Pickled Beets
Sautéed Spinach
Red Beans and Rice
Sautéed Squash, Cabbage, and Zucchini
Stewed Tomatoes
Tobacco Onion Rings
Turnip Greens
White Beans (Dry)

Breads   135

ABOUT THE AUTHOR

Martha lives outside of Nashville, Tennessee, with her husband, John. Cooking is her go-to activity for feeling good with the familiar. She sold cakes when she was a single young mother because everyone would ask her to bake for them. Later, Martha owned and operated a barbeque and catering place with her husband.

Though she loves cooking, she also finds much pleasure in painting, both acrylic and oils. With her art, Martha doesn't just produce artworks; she celebrates color. Very few of her works are intentional. Her themes and the subjects that she puts on canvas are all over the place. Martha looks forward to having a showing of all her works one day.

When Martha is not cooking or painting, she is sewing. Martha's family usually celebrates with food. The bigger the spread, the better—a little of everything with something for everyone.

Martha has a lot of inspiration to draw from and hopes to share that energy in some of her pages. Her number one tester is her husband. Of course, Martha's mother can never find any fault with her cooking, so she does rely on feedback from friends and relatives. Martha hopes you find something delicious in this book to add to your favorite dishes.

Printed in the USA
CPSIA information can be obtained
at www.ICGtesting.com
LVHW072156261023
762248LV00013B/196